# Frontier
# Physician

# Frontier Physician

## The Life and Legacy of
## Dr. C. Earl Albrecht

*Dr. C. Earl Albrecht heads out on a housecall in 1935.*

# Nancy Jordan

## Foreword by Robert B. Atwood

Epicenter Press
Fairbanks/Seattle

Publication of this book was made possible through underwriting and support from the Albrecht-Milan Foundation of the American Society for Circumpolar Health, working toward providing better health services and understanding the unique health problems of the polar regions.

Editor: Sue Mattson
Cover design: Elizabeth Watson
Cover illustration: Gail Niebrugge
Inside design: Sue Mattson
Maps: Rusty Nelson
Proofreader: Delisa Clendendon
Printer: Best Books Manufacturing

Library of Congress Cataloging-in-Publication Data
Jordan. Nancy, 1923-
    Frontier physician : the life and legacy of Dr. C. Earl Albrecht / Nancy Jordan ; foreword by Bob Atwood
        p. cm.
    Includes bibliographical references and index.
    ISBN 0-945397-52-6 (hbk.). -- ISBN 0-945397-50-X (pbk.)
    1. Albrecht, C. Earl. 2. Physicians--Alaska--Biography. 3. Medical care--Alaska--History. 4. Indians of North America--Medical care--Alaska--History. I. Title.
R154.A39J67 1996
610'.92--dc20
[B]                                                                96-637
                                                                   CIP

Photos: All photos courtesy of the C. Earl and Margery J. Albrecht Collection, except as follows: title page photo courtesy Max Sherrod; Chapter 6 (page 83) photo courtesy Alaska Department of Health; Chapter 8 (page 111) photo courtesy Alaska State Library, Department of Health and Social Services Collection; Chapter 14 (page 193) photo courtesy Leda Milan.

To order single copies of FRONTIER PHYSICIAN, mail $14.95 each (Washington residents add $1.23 sales tax) plus $4.00 for shipping to: Epicenter Press, Box 82368, Kenmore, WA 98028.
Booksellers: Retail discounts are available from our trade distributor, Graphic Arts Center Publishing™. Box 10306. Portland, OR 97210. Phone 800-452-3032.

First Printing April 1996
10 9 8 7 6 5 4 3 2 1

Printed in Canada

# Table of Contents

# Foreword

This is the story of C. Earl Albrecht, a young physician from Pennsylvania who came to Alaska in 1935 and in twenty-one years became one of the great men in the history of the North.

On his arrival, Albrecht played a vital role in federal colonization of the Matanuska Valley. During World War II he was in command of the territory's main military hospital. Alaska was then the only warfront where the enemy occupied U.S. soil. After the war Albrecht became territorial commissioner of health, a position he held for eleven years.

In each of the three areas of service his performance was extraordinary. In the Matanuska Valley he stamped out childhood illnesses, delivered hundreds of babies and for many years was the sole physician to the entire frontier settlement. In those days families were crowded in tent houses. Living conditions were austere.

During the war he operated the first hospital built at Fort Richardson, and was responsible for the health care of as many as 50,000 troops.

After his military service, Gov. Ernest Gruening tapped him to be territorial commissioner of health and challenged him to stop the plague of tuberculosis then rampant among the Native population.

He all but eradicated tuberculosis and in doing so made himself Alaska's equivalent to Dr. W.C. Gorgas, who wiped out malaria and scarlet fever to make possible construction of the Panama Canal.

Albrecht's vision and concern for all people of the north inspired him to establish what has become the International Union for Circumpolar Health. His efforts brought together for the first time physicians and scientists who deal with people of the arctic regions and their health. Today, it is a flourishing organization serving the top of the world.

Albrecht's success in raising living standards of all Alaskans should give him a permanent place among Alaska's great leaders such as Governor Gruening, Sen. E.L. "Bob" Bartlett, and Judge James Wickersham.

Robert B. Atwood

# Preface

I have always been a planner. While still a youngster, I believed in looking ahead and envisioning my life. It seemed an important way for me to keep control of my fate, to use my days wisely. But as I grew older I noticed that my path sometimes went in unexpected directions. Although I fulfilled my intent to become a Moravian clergyman, for example, it gave way to my becoming a physician. My determination to serve the Native community in Bethel, Alaska, was undone by my assignment to the haphazard colony in Palmer. And life continued to take sharp detours. What was happening, I wondered. Of what value was all my serious and well-considered planning?

What was happening was that God was a far better designer of my life than I was, and with this awareness all my efforts became more rewarding than I could have hoped. In all manner of situations, happy and unhappy, I have had my ally and my guide. Whenever I have sought God's counsel, He has given it to me; when I have needed energy and wisdom, He has supplied it.

In the following pages are accounts of some of my achievements but they are by no means mine alone. Through divine blessing I have been given countless people to help me serve my causes. Among these I bow to the magnificent Native Alaskans I came to know and work with. I owe much to them. And through divine grace I have been given the gifts of my family, my wife Margery, to whom I dedicate this story of my life, and my children, Jane, Jack and Linda. In gratitude for God's enduring guidance and benevolence, I have tried to make my career and my life a testimony to the partnership I have ever had with my Lord.

*C. Earl Albrecht, M.D.*

C. Earl Albrecht, M.D.

# Acknowledgments

In his remarkable journey from pioneer doctor to international health expert, C. Earl Albrecht amassed a small army of devoted admirers—and, yes, a few critics—who hold cherished memories of him and his exceptional achievements. To the many who shared those memories with me, I am greatly indebted, especially to the nurses he worked with in Palmer, his Anchorage cohorts of territorial days, and those who joined his train in his later years and gratefully learned from him.

Max Sherrod, Stella Odsather, Bob Atwood, Helen Beirne, Leda Milan, Claire Kopperud, Gerry Keeling, Carl Hild, Drs. John and Betsy Tower, Miriam Hilscher, Mary Bagoy Lakshas, William Graffius, and Elmer Rasmuson all contributed in special ways to telling the Albrecht story. Lyle Perrigo put me in touch with priceless tapes and knowledgeable people.

Dr. Robert Fortuine and Dr. John Middaugh directed me down fruitful paths and patiently and graciously clarified my syntax and my facts. Dr. Robert Smith and Dr. Lee Gehrig supplied important recollections of the tuberculosis campaign. Dr. Frank Pauls, Lois Jund, and Kitty Gair are three obliging souls from Earl's commissioner days who untiringly endured and answered many questions. Earl's sister, Mrs. Gertrude Teufer, was a fount of family memorabilia, and his daughter, Mrs. Jane Graf, filled in her father's wartime years.

Board members of the Albrecht-Milan Foundation, who commissioned the writing of this book for the Tenth International Congress on Circumpolar Health, were staunch and enthusiastic supporters. Jeff Barber in the office of U.S. Senator Ted Stevens and Eleanor Roser in the office of State Representative Ramona Barnes fulfilled requests kindly and efficiently.

The staff of the archives at the Consortium Library of the University of Alaska Anchorage, with Dennis Walle's fine cooperation, was always at the ready with their valuable files. Their colleagues at the Elmer E. Rasmuson Library of the University of Alaska Fairbanks, especially William Schneider, and at the State of Alaska Archives in Juneau , notably Kathryn H. Shelton, also were proficient and quick to assist.

Bruce Merrell, Alaska bibliographer in the Alaska Collection at the Z. J. Loussac Public Library in Anchorage, unearthed important military accounts of World War II days in the territory. Dr. Darniel R. Gilbert, archivist, and Bertie F. Knisely at Moravian College dug deep and profitably in their records.

I had the exceptional advantage of having, in my house, perhaps the nation's best editor, my Pulitzer-Prize winning husband, John Strohmeyer. When he approved my work, I could move on to further writing—but only then. At my right hand, ever accommodating and diligent in research, has been Earl's worshipful wife, Margery. She enabled me to document this book by sharing, with dispatch and good humor, exhaustive materials from the voluminous Albrecht files in their Florida garage. It is possible this book could have been written without her help, but it is difficult to see how.

Nancy Jordan

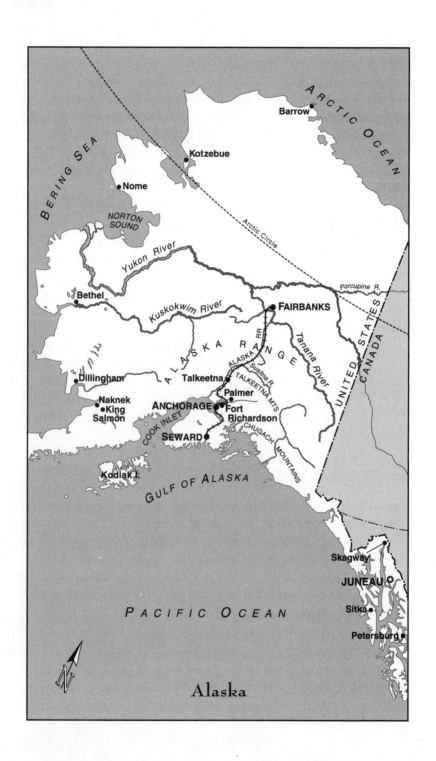

Alaska

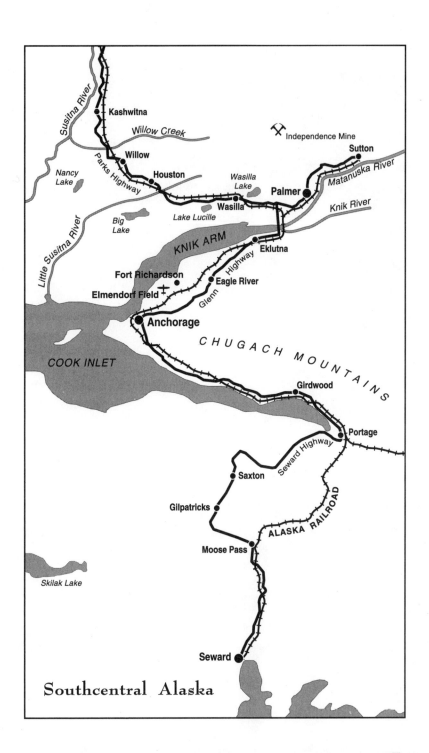

Southcentral Alaska

# CHAPTER 1
# Palmer Colony

*Dr. Albrecht writes a prescription for a patient
in the Palmer colony in 1935.*

W hen the hospital phone rang for the fifth time,
the weary doctor conceded, reluctantly, that the
caller was not about to quit. Earl Albrecht could only hope
it was not an emergency calling him away from a heavy
schedule. But, of course, it had to mean trouble. People in
this remote part of Southcentral Alaska took care of their
own ailments whenever they could. Tough, resolute, independent farmers, they asked for help only during a crisis.

Albrecht looked around for a nurse to take the call but
his meager staff was busy with patients. With resignation

he picked up the phone. He was startled to hear the soft
voice of a young girl.

"Please, doctor, you've got to come right away. Mama's
awful sick."

"What's wrong?" Albrecht asked. "Who are you? And
where are you?"

"I'm up here in Sutton. I'm Mrs. Ezi's daughter." Then
the voice dropped. "I can't tell you what's wrong." There
was a pause. "Please. Just come."

Ezi . . . Sutton . . . Albrecht tried to make a mental
connection. He had no patients in Sutton, a small mining
community about eleven miles north of his modest hospital in the Palmer colony. Reachable only by the Alaska Railroad, Sutton consisted of a few miners and Athabaskan
Indians of the Chickaloon tribe.

The doctor was baffled. He knew this was no ordinary
summons. The girl had to be Indian, and Indians seldom
called a doctor for help.

"You'll have to tell me what's wrong," the doctor said
insistently. "I can't leave here unless I know what is the
matter."

The voice hesitated, then dropped to a whisper. "She
can't pee," the girl said. "She hasn't been able to for a
long, long time."

Then it came to him. Almost as soon as he had arrived
at the railroad hospital in Anchorage several weeks earlier,
having just finished his internship, Albrecht had been given
the assignment of operating on an Indian woman with
advanced cancer.

"Let the new fellow do it," the medical director had
said. And he had. Albrecht had removed a tumor in her
bowel, and in due time the director had sent the patient
home. He recalled she lived in Sutton with her children
and husband. But he had heard nothing of her since then.

"Where are you calling from?" he asked. Members of
the Chickaloon tribe, he knew, were impoverished, living

modestly in crude cabins and huts. Telephones were beyond their means.

"I'm at the railroad office," said the young voice, and
Albrecht felt a flash of remorse, knowing she was embar-
rassed to explain her mother's condition in a public place.
"Wait for me. I'll be there," Albrecht said. "It'll take a
while but I'll come as soon as I can. Tell your mother that."

Coming as soon as he could, back then in 1935, de-
pended on the railroad, which operated on its own time
and often at a snail's pace. Albrecht called the station and
asked for a section car to Sutton as soon as one was available. Then, after leaving patients' orders, he summoned a
nurse to pack his bag and announced he was not sure when
he would be back.

The slow, bumpy ride through the glowing August
evening gave Albrecht, then thirty, a chance to reflect on
the path his vocation had taken. In medical school in the
early '30s, he had set his heart on treating Natives—Eskimos, Indians, Aleuts—in Alaska's Bush, an ambition apro-
pos to his Moravian Church missionary heritage. It was
not to be. Soon after arriving in Anchorage, he had been
ordered to report to the fledgling farming community of
Palmer, 40 miles to the north. Although there was no road
to the settlement, only the sluggish railroad, it was hardly
the Bush he had set his heart on serving.

Awaiting him in Palmer were not the Natives he had
hoped to help but a hapless group of 202 white families
from failed farms of Minnesota, Michigan and Wisconsin.
It was President Franklin D. Roosevelt's bold plan to establish the farmers, victims of the Great Depression, in what
he believed could become an Alaska breadbasket. Temperatures in Palmer were not so different from the Great Lakes
states, the reasoning went, and the move would give the
destitute settlers a new start. And Alaska could use the
stable population.

Albrecht was excited to be in Palmer, much as he was

excited to be in Alaska, but he carried a faint regret that
his youthful dreams had not been fulfilled. When he had
an opportunity to help a Native, as he did tonight, it was
particular satisfying for him to do so.

A railroad worker pointed the way to a small cabin at
the edge of a grassy field when the train pulled into Sutton.
Albrecht headed down the narrow path and into the cabin.
The interior was dim but he could see the family gathered
to console a bedridden woman covered by a sheet. Immediately he recognized his first Alaska surgical patient.
Lighted candles surrounded her.

Even before he removed the sheet, Albrecht knew the
woman's distress. Her moaning, severely extended stomach, and contorted face told of her suffering. Her cancer
had returned in full. The doctor washed his hands in a pail
of rainwater and then turned to his bag for a catheter to
release what he knew was a blocked bladder. To his horror,
he could find no catheter.

"It must be in here," he muttered as he dug frantically
through the bag. Mentally he blamed himself for not check-
ing the equipment and the nurse for not packing a catheter. The woman's family watched silently, taking in his
search. In exasperation, Albrecht rose from the woman's
side and appraised the situation.

He stepped from the crowded cabin out into the fresh
Alaska air to escape the family and to consider his op-
tions. He could send back to the hospital for a catheter but
that would take hours and he was sadly aware of the
woman's agony.

He could try to fashion a tube of sorts from the enema
equipment—in Anchorage he had had to construct a makeshift tube for a blood transfusion—but it would lack the
necessary rigidity. There was nothing in his bag nor could
he see anything in the meager dwelling he could use.

In the distance the magnificent Talkeetna Mountains

still bore gleaming traces of snow, but Albrecht was beyond appreciating their beauty now. The persistent
Matanuska Valley wind whirled glacial dust around his
boots and the field of grasses before him rose and fell in
waves.

Suddenly the scene brought to mind a boyhood
memory. Growing up on his father's farm in Minnesota,
he and his brother had hollowed out just such grasses and
blown water at one another. Could he use one of these
reeds now to relieve the woman's misery?

Eagerly, he pulled up several stalks. The season's long,
sunny days and an unusual summer drought had left them
dry and firm. The Lord must have planted these here for
me to use, he thought. It might work. Why not try? There
seemed to be no ready alternative.

He ran back to the hut with a few of the stalks, reamed
them out, found antiseptic in his bag and made them as
clean as possible. Then carefully, gently, he inserted a reed
into the woman's urethra.

Almost immediately a yellow stream arced through the
air and splashed on the cabin floor. Albrecht breathed a
silent prayer of thanks; with a hollow straw he had opened
the clogged bladder. The doctor's audience clapped and
cheered in admiration but he took his reward in the relief
gradually replacing misery on the woman's face.

"Show me how to do that," the woman's husband
pleaded. Albrecht had to smile. Perhaps the use of a reed
looked like a trick anyone could do, but the procedure was
honed in years of medical school and interning.

"No, Mr. Ezi, I think you'd better leave it up to me if
she needs it again," he said.

The doctor's success was bittersweet, however. While
release and joy reigned inside the cabin, Albrecht feared
the patient's prognosis was not good. The new blockage
was a sinister development. Still, he felt the jubilation of

relieving a patient's pain, and he chuckled because he had done it with a boyhood diversion.

His euphoria survived the return trip, and although he arrived late at the hospital he recounted the event to his staff with relish.

Claire Kopperud, a seasoned nurse working the night shift, was tickled by his elation. "Don't think he didn't enjoy every minute of that," she confided to a fellow nurse. "That's just the kind of challenge he likes."

Alaska had been sending challenges Albrecht's way almost from the day he arrived in the territory. Nothing had gone as planned, yet he had a knack of turning minuses into pluses. He refused to let disappointment get in his way. He adjusted.

It surely had not been his plan to use his medical skills in a white farming community. He had envisioned his future in Bethel, a Yupik village in western Alaska where his fellow Moravians had established a mission. The Moravian Church, a Protestant denomination founded in 1457 in what is now the Czech Republic, had a long heritage in medical missionary service to indigenous people, and Albrecht wanted to be part of it.

In Bethel, as elsewhere in rural Alaska in the '30s, the federal Bureau of Indian Affairs was in charge of the Natives' health care. While still a student at Jefferson Medical College in Philadelphia, Albrecht had pestered the BIA and Anthony Dimond, Alaska's sole territorial representative in Washington, D.C., for assignment to Bethel.

"You will go there when we get a hospital built there," the BIA told him. Dimond made the same promise to the eager young man. But the hospital's construction was repeatedly postponed.

Then Dr. Joseph Romig, also a Moravian and known to Albrecht, offered him a position at the Anchorage Railroad Hospital where Romig was the medical director. It wasn't

Bethel but at least it would put Albrecht within reach of the village. He accepted wholeheartedly.

Anchorage was still a frontier town when Albrecht stepped off the train from Seward in June 1935. Fewer than twenty-five hundred people lived there, mostly in tiny cottages heated by wood stoves. Indians roamed the gravel roadways; sidewalks—where there were sidewalks—were the wooden ones he had seen only in western movies. There was just one public place to eat and that was more diner than restaurant.

All commerce centered around the Alaska Railroad, which ran from the port of Seward to the Interior city of Fairbanks with branches to a few mining areas. Anchorage gave no hint then of the prosperous urban hub it was to become. It was simply a fair-sized stop on the railroad.

Still, it was a promising stop. Albrecht was impressed with what he described in letters home as "wonderful people making this place develop into something permanent." Permanence had not been a hallmark of Alaska's population. The territory, still more than twenty years from becoming a state, attracted mainly hit-and-run adventurers who came to seek a fortune, seldom succeeded and soon moved on.

No wonder, Albrecht reflected, the city had made a festive welcome for FDR's transplanted midwestern families who passed through on their way to Palmer in May 1935. Their story had invigorated depression-weary America. Here were farmers whose livelihoods had been lost to the financial disaster shared by the entire nation. Now they were gathering their fortitude and hopes to make their future in Palmer in Alaska's Matanuska Valley (wherever that was, many wondered) and to turn it into a bountiful garden.

Roosevelt had promised the government would give each family forty acres, a modern home, financial support,

schools, a hospital, plus all the farm equipment they needed
in exchange for their promise to develop the land. Applicants were expected to have the necessary skills, to be
physically fit and to have a pioneering spirit. Competition
for the opportunity was brisk.

Some in Alaska criticized the federal project, saying if
it failed the territory would have a host of indigents on its
hands. But others were more optimistic. For years scientists in Palmer's small Experimental Farm Station had been
touting the agricultural possibilities of the valley. M. D.
Snodgrass, a director of the station, personally had persuaded a dozen families to move in as homesteaders. Robert B. Atwood, publisher of the *Anchorage Daily Times*, saw
the FDR company as a boon, a stabilizing force.

However, in the Lower 48, as Alaskans referred to the
continental United States, bureaucracy took over the operation. The selection system was rushed and slipshod;
important conditions of the contracts often went unex-
plained and were misunderstood. The successful applicants
irrationally were given to believe they had won the equivalent of the Irish sweepstakes. One, who apparently failed
to consult a map, even arrived with golf clubs.

Nevertheless, residents of Alaska, particularly Anchorage, believed the territory finally was attracting long-over-
due recognition. The city was proud to have the honor of
introducing the colonists to their new community.

The settlers had arrived about a month before Albrecht
had settled in at Anchorage, and they now were trying to
get used to life in tents as they awaited construction of
their homes. The doctor also was trying to get used to his
new surroundings. When Romig threw him the task of re-
moving the Indian woman's malignant tumor, he had been
on duty just a week. Albrecht, who had won a surgery
prize at Jefferson, expected to do surgery but was surprised
by the hospital's antiquated procedures.

"Where's the blood-transfusion equipment?" he asked Romig as he prepared for the operation.

"Blood transfusion? We don't do that here. We don't give blood transfusions," Romig replied.

"I can't operate unless I know I can give a blood transfusion if I have to," Albrecht said firmly.

"Well, we have nothing here," Romig said. "But you'll have to do the surgery. This patient won't make it without removal of that blockage."

Nothing here, Albrecht thought. I'll just have to make something on my own.

He made his way to the laboratory and looked around for anything that could be turned into an intravenous application. Romig had been right—there was nothing. Well, almost nothing. Albrecht noticed a collection of lengths of tubing. When he finished putting them together with an intravenous needle, he had fashioned the Railroad Hospital's first blood-transfusion equipment. His luck continued when he found a hospital employee who the lab determined had the right blood type and who agreed to donate the blood.

That challenge met and conquered, Alaska gave Albrecht another and more significant one only two weeks later. The doctor had started typing a letter to his mother in Bethlehem, Pennsylvania, the night of July 12, 1935, when Romig walked into his office. A glance at the director's grave demeanor told Albrecht something serious was coming.

"Earl, things are bad in the valley," Romig said. "I want you to go out there tonight and take care of those colonists. Children are sick, there have been three deaths, the people are frantic and there's an investigating team from Washington that's insisting we do something immediately."

"Tonight?" Albrecht echoed. "But there's no way I can get there. There's no train."

"There'll be a train," Romig said. "I've already arranged with Colonel Ohlson for the use of the Speeder to get you there."

Things must really be bad in Palmer, Albrecht thought. Col. Otto F. Ohlson, manager of the railroad, did not readily offer the use of the Speeder, a Dodge sedan outfitted with locomotive wheels and the special delight of the manager.

Albrecht had known all was not well with the farm families. The modern homes had not been ready as promised; everyone was living in tents, hauling water, burying wastes and growing more angry by the day. But that was not the worst of it. The grumbling had turned into fear when three babies died of infectious diseases within weeks after arrival.

After Agnes Sandvik, a colonist's wife, wrote Eleanor Roosevelt the dire news that the babies had died from lack of medical care, an official delegation was dispatched immediately. The members had interviewed Albrecht and the hospital's third physician, Dr. A. S. Walkowski, on their way to Palmer. The meeting had been pleasant enough but when Romig and Ohlson took the delegation to the colony where distraught parents were assembled and making demands, the investigators turned flinty. Get a doctor up here immediately, they ordered sternly.

A Red Cross nurse and two other registered nurses—a married couple, Max and Dorothy Sherrod—had accompanied the colonists from Seattle to Palmer. Many of the children had contracted severe infectious diseases, and in the close confines of travel, illness surged through the younger population.

The Sherrods' responsibilities ended with their arrival in Palmer, leaving the Red Cross nurse, Madeleine deForas, to provide the colony's sole medical care. For weeks she had spent her days and most of her nights going from tent to tent to care for the sick children as parental concern mounted. With the only hospital a day's train ride away in

Anchorage and no physician on hand, the three deaths had sent the disorganized community into full panic.

Albrecht rose and covered the typewriter, his letter home temporarily abandoned. Together he and Romig worked out a plan. Three nurses and Albrecht with as many supplies as could be collected would head for the colony as soon as possible. They would stay as long as needed.

Even as he recognized the demands of the emergency, Albrecht feared for his long-held plans. "I hope this won't prevent me from going to Bethel," he said to Romig in what was more question than statement.

"Earl, you're needed right now in Palmer," Romig said. "You can go to Bethel later." But it would be many eventful years before Albrecht would see Bethel, and then not as he might have expected.

Samuel R. Fuller, who headed the investigating team, had ordered the colony's community building be converted to a hospital. The one existing frame building, it had only three enclosed sides; in honor of the valley's annual mosquito infestation, the fourth side was screened. Then he ordered construction of a new hospital to begin at once. Fuller himself took over temporary supervision of the colony from Don L. Irwin, the manager.

By midnight, a baggage car had been loaded in Anchorage with cots, mattresses, linens and an abundance of medical supplies and medicine. Joining Albrecht on the Speeder were nurses Lillian Mills, Mary Bagoy, and Katherine Powers.

The doctor's usual geniality failed him on the train ride, nor were the nurses in a conversational mood. Too many troublesome questions lingered unanswered, not the least of which was just how widespread were the infections. Do we have an epidemic on our hands, the four wondered. Riding through the soft summer night, Albrecht turned quietly to prayer.

Although it was approaching 2 a.m. when the Speeder

pulled into the Matanuska station, anxious parents were
waiting somberly. Albrecht scanned the faces for signs of
anger but saw only gratitude.

"I could feel everyone heave a sigh of relief," he later
wrote home. "There had been much fear and tension among
the colonists because they didn't have medical help. The
peace and calm we were able to give impressed me and I'll
never forget it all my life. It was not that I had any special
qualities. It was that they trusted us and we represented
the medical profession. The thanks we received were very
warm and enduring."

To the colonists, the team from Anchorage might have
descended from heaven rather than from Colonel Ohlson's
Speeder. The nurses, Mary Bagoy and Katherine Powers,
young and earnest, and Lillian Mills, middle-aged and
staunch, looked like a trio of angels in their crisp white
uniforms and perky caps.

Albrecht, slight of stature and gentle by nature, was
not an imposing figure. His benign, handsome face reflected
more compassion than authority. But he carried the
physician's black bag, and the colonists all but bowed in
homage. Never, he told himself with an inward chuckle,
underestimate the power of the stethoscope.

Carpenters framed in the community building's fourth
wall as cots were set up. The first patient, a child with
uncontrolled asthma and measles, was admitted at 5 a.m.
Within a few hours others with chicken pox and scarlet
fever had filled the ten beds. Sheets were hung from the
ceiling to provide isolation of a sort, a drum of water was
positioned next to a sink, two woodstoves were stoked to
keep the patients warm, and Palmer had its first hospital.

And Albrecht had his first assignment as a medical director. For once, he began to think perhaps he was not
destined for Bethel after all.

# CHAPTER 2
# Frontier Hospital

*Dr. Albrecht sets out
for a housecall by horseback.*

Early in September 1935, Albrecht made one of his rare trips to Anchorage. For two months, his life had consisted of total immersion in the colony's health care. His long days at the hospital had blended into evenings, and evenings into early mornings. When not treating patients or managing his staff, he was hunched over plans for the new hospital the Department of the Interior had authorized after the federal inspection.

He was chipper as he climbed aboard the train for its daily run to Anchorage—with good reason. He was on his way to his wedding.

When Albrecht returned to Palmer six days later, he
was wearing a broad grin, carrying a box of cigars, and
sporting a bride on his arm. The colony was elated. And
curious.

While interning at Abington Memorial Hospital outside
Philadelphia, Albrecht had worked with a nurse, Blanche
Smith, who supervised the operating room. They had developed a closeness that was so guarded few were aware
of it. Her assistant, Ruth Kelly, told people later, "It was a
very quiet courtship." Only his mother knew of the ro-
mance.

Before Albrecht left for Alaska, he and Blanche discussed marrying after he was settled in at Anchorage. But
when Albrecht found himself in the struggling community
of Palmer, he began to doubt whether it was the place for a
bride, particularly one from the East.

"This is not an easy life here," he wrote Blanche. "I
live in a tent with a wood stove and although it is temporary there is no guarantee when I will get more permanent
quarters. There is no indoor plumbing or electricity and
winter is coming on. From what I've heard, that's a challenge in itself. If you would rather wait until spring, I will
understand."

Blanche, however, was undeterred. She set out on the
long train ride across the United States, boarded the boat
at Seattle for Seward and then the train for Anchorage,
arriving there on September 6, 1935. Earl met her, carrying
an armful of flowers. He wondered what her reaction would
be to Alaska and its rugged frontier atmosphere.

Blanche had scant time to notice her surroundings. After
changing into a new blue suit, she was whisked off to the
First Presbyterian Church to be married. She had been in
Anchorage all of one hour.

It was probably not the fine wedding the bride might
have wished for, but it was a proper one. The groom, in

his typical fashion, had given careful attention to details and was determined to provide a fitting ritual, even if it was in a rustic Alaska town. His good friend and mentor, Dr. Romig, officiated with the assistance of the pastor, the Rev. E. L. Winterberger. The couple was attended by Dr. Romig's son, Robert, and by Katherine Powers, one of Albrecht's nurses in Palmer.

Albrecht had arranged for a wedding march, played by Helen Welsh of Anchorage, and even a soloist, Robert S. Bragaw, who sang, "I Love You Truly."

Following the Moravian ceremony, the wedding party adjourned to the Romigs' home where a festive dinner awaited. Then the newlyweds were off to the Romigs' summer cabin for their honeymoon.

Such were marriages in Alaska in the 1930s. When a bride-to-be arrived in town, the ceremony was performed as quickly as possible, usually out of consideration for propriety.

Families were almost always far away and the couples had to make their own arrangements. The Albrecht ceremony included more tradition than most.

Albrecht was proud to show off Alaska to his bride, pointing out Mount McKinley's gleaming crown on the northern horizon, the spectacular Alaska Range, and the ever-changing Cook Inlet. But he was chafing to return to Palmer.

If he had known what was in store, he might not have been so eager. The colony's greeting was to plunk Blanche into a wheelbarrow and insist that her new husband wheel her to their tent home, paying no mind to the bride's startled objections. Blanche endured the bumpy ride with her innate gentility but Albrecht was painfully aware of her discomfort.

"Don't worry, Doc," a man in the welcoming party called out cheerfully. "This is an old Wisconsin custom."

It was not the kind of reception Albrecht had hoped for, however. The following evening a band of youngsters arrived outside the Albrecht tent, blowing whistles, banging on pans, and making a racket. The chagrined doctor finally slipped Jimmy Moore, a colonist, six dollars to get the noisy crowd off his front yard and down to the government store for candy.

The newlyweds hadn't escaped yet. The next night a large crowd of grinning adult couples demanded that the Albrechts treat them to ice cream—no one was quite certain where that custom originated—and this time the bill was considerably higher. Quite a traumatic initiation for his bride, Earl thought—a one-room tent, an outhouse, mud streets, and rowdy strangers.

What Albrecht considered far more disturbing was the seething anger and frustration that had risen from the moment the farm families had stepped off the train and seen the close line-up of white tents where they were to live until permanent frame homes were built. This was hardly the picture of a comfortable life in the Matanuska Valley the government had drawn for them.

The Alaska Rural Rehabilitation Corporation, known as ARRC, was established by the Department of the Interior to manage the colony. Don L. Irwin, who had been an employee of the Palmer Experimental Farm Station, became its first manager and soon found he had a tough assignment.

The entire project had been planned hastily and haphazardly by federal bureaucrats with little understanding of Alaska. Many members of Congress had opposed the colony from the beginning, and it was starting to appear their opposition was justified.

The Department of the Interior, headed by Harold Ickes, and the newly formed Federal Emergency Relief Administration, headed by Harry Hopkins, were given joint responsibility but little time to set up the colony. On April 26, 1935, only three months after the project was approved, selected Minnesota families boarded the train at St. Paul bound for the West Coast. Less than three weeks later, the Michigan and Wisconsin contingents were on their way. Unfortunately, it was the time of year in Alaska when winter dies slowly and construction plans wait on paper.

As the colonists headed for their new lives, their spirits were high. Many had lived in dwellings that were little more than shacks on impoverished farms. Now they were leaving that behind, heading for the promise of a free paradise. Adding to their intoxication were the overwhelming receptions they received along the route. Gifts of food, clothing, and toys were piled on them by cheering crowds. For the first heady time in their lives, the families experienced luxury, such as their quarters in San Francisco's Mark Hopkins Hotel.

The festive mood vanished by the time the men lined up in Palmer on May 23, 1935, for the critical property lottery. Each of the two hundred and two Midwest farmers and their families hoped to be lucky enough to draw a choice tract of land. And if it could be along a salmon stream . . . well, that was almost too much to ask.

Inevitably, the assignment of land tracts disappointed some. But all were disappointed, and vocally so, in the housing. A California-based Civilian Conservation Corps had been contracted to build the homes, but first the land had to be cleared, foundations dug, and materials imported. Due to conflicting policies in the ARRC and in Washington, little of the work was taking place. It was painfully clear the inconvenient tent life was going to continue for quite a while.

By Independence Day, six families had given up and returned to the states.

Shipping delays, mixed-up orders, and insufficient

numbers of workers stifled building progress, and summer
was slipping away fast. The farmers begged for the right to
build their own houses, but they were turned down since
the corps had a contract.

The Fuller investigating committee arrived in July to
address the problems. With the appointment of new ARRC
personnel and the addition of extra laborers (including some
resident Alaskans), houses finally began to go up.

For some of the colonists, the sluggish progress was
too late. There had been too much frustration, red tape,
and worry about getting under cover before snow fell. The
prices at the commissary were too high and the governmental rules too oppressive, the colonists complained. With
the tragic deaths of the three children—on June 20, July 7,
and July 9—the growing sense of helplessness and rage
deepened. Before the end of August, although thirty-six
homes were completed and one hundred forty more were
under construction, forty families had abandoned the
colony.

And it was becoming obvious some Midwest welfare
agencies had used the Palmer project to rid their files of
troublesome families. Not only had they approved chronic
complainers but also those with major health problems—
even one with a wooden leg—who would find frontier life
far too difficult. Albrecht, assigned to assess such cases,
sent forty more families back to their Midwest homes.

Palmer hadn't turned out to be what Albrecht expected,
either, but he saw he was too desperately needed to quit.
His daily line of patients attested to that. Furthermore, the
missionary fire still burned within him. He had come to
the frontier to use his medical skills for healing, and although he had treated few Natives, he was convinced God
had brought him to the right place.

Another factor also kept Albrecht in the valley. That
was his admiration for those colonists who accepted the

hardships and turned them into accomplishments. Their trust in an Alaska future and their willingness to work toward it struck him as noble. He found it encouraging that these people were in the majority, and he was certain they would become productive Alaskans.

He was less sure he was up to handling the sole responsibility for the settlement's health care. In emergencies he could turn to Dr. Romig, but that help was forty miles and nearly two hours away. "I was the only doctor," he recalled later, "and I shudder at the things I had to do."

He was grateful he had taken many extra courses at Jefferson Medical College in anticipation of service in the Bush. They had been a drain on his energies at the time, but, as a result, he was able to perform surgery, read x-rays, conduct lab work, give blood transfusions, use the intravenous therapy—just coming into practice—and assemble supplies and equipment.

He was also lucky, a hallmark that became something of an Albrecht legend. What others considered luck, though, he attributed to "divine providence."

He was fortunate, for example, that Max and Dorothy Sherrod, both nurses, were in Palmer. The Sherrods, like the colonists, were seeking a way out of the depression for themselves and their three-year-old daughter, Janet. From their home in Battle Creek, Michigan, they, too, had headed west to Seattle, and when the Alaska Railroad representative there learned of their skills, he offered them free passage in exchange for their nursing services en route.

Once in Palmer, the Sherrods settled into a tent and planted a garden. Max took a job as laborer at the warehouse. But both soon were drafted by Albrecht to help at the makeshift hospital. Max, outgoing and quick-witted, proved to be an invaluable asset to the doctor, and Dorothy, calm and petite, took charge of the separate maternity tent.

"At the beginning, things were pretty rough," Sherrod recalled later. "We had no routine facilities, such as heat, electricity, water, toilets. A bulldozed hole with a covered wood opening was used for any form of waste material from the hospital. The walls of the building were badly cracked, and dust from the Matanuska River bed seemed to blow in everywhere.

"The only artificial light came from gasoline lanterns. The nurses were so afraid of them I or some other man had to light them. Dorothy and I loaned our personal pressure cooker for sterilizing. The only heat came from wood stoves. The doctor and I together chopped the wood for them.

"I had to see that water was on hand. Everyone had to haul their own water from wells a half-mile away, a darned heavy job, so I rigged up a system. I got two fifty-gallon steel barrels and put them on a raised platform and filled them with water which was piped into a sink near the stove. This was wonderful as then we could wash hands and get the patients water."

Sherrod and Albrecht worked well together from the beginning, a partnership that met its first medical challenge when Lucille Ring, a fourteen-year-old, was brought to the hospital with a high fever on August 8, 1935. Within hours she became completely paralyzed from her neck to her toes.

"Dr. Albrecht diagnosed her condition as either poliomyelitis or meningitis," Sherrod said. "All the doctor had was an outdated vial of meningeal serum which we had to use because there wasn't anything else available, even in Anchorage."

Albrecht had been in the colony for less than a month when this crisis occurred but he already had learned to make do with what was on hand. He had Sherrod hold the patient in a position for spinal injections as he put the expired serum to use with a needle and a prayer. Although Sherrod thought it a rather unorthodox procedure, he realized it was another example of the ingenuity frontier medicine required.

Albrecht feared the case might not be an isolated one. The girl was given the hospital's sheet-curtain quarantine, and the staff rejoiced as she slowly recovered with no ill effects. Lucille's clearest memory of the event is the bicycle and the yarn she received from Colonel Ohlson, the railroad manager. During her convalescence she used the yarn to make potholders.

Outdated serum, sheets for isolation, and a pressure cooker for sterilization must be what's meant by frontier medicine, Albrecht told himself. Perhaps there should be a medical school course in "How to Improvise in the Bush." The idea resurfaced the night a woman was brought to the hospital with an ectopic pregnancy, in which the fertilized egg becomes implanted in a Fallopian tube rather than the uterus. As the fetus grows, the tube ruptures, causing internal bleeding.

The situation is always dangerous, and in this case it was decidedly so. During surgery, Albrecht found the abdominal cavity filled with blood.

"Collect as much of her blood as you can," Albrecht told a nurse. "We don't have time to match it, we'll just have to put it back in her."

"What about these clots?" the nurse asked worriedly.

Albrecht paused for a moment. "See if you can find some cheesecloth," he said. "Max may have some. Strain it through the cheesecloth."

The nurse gave him a startled glance but left without comment to search for Max Sherrod. From his motley storeroom Sherrod produced a length of cheesecloth and sterilized it in the pressure cooker.

Later, after his patient was out of danger, Albrecht sat

down to write his report. His notes evolved in standard
professional form until he came to the matter of the cheesecloth. Here he stopped and then, throwing back his head,
burst into laughter. Two nurses working in the ward heard
him and rolled their eyes at each other.

How I'd love to send a copy of this to Jefferson and
Abington, he thought gleefully. He pictured his staid Eastern colleagues gasping at the account. Maybe I'll tell them
about the reed that became a catheter, too, he thought. But
as he picked up his pen to finish his report, he knew he
would never send it on to Philadelphia. It was too bizarre
to be believed.

The risks he ran with inadequate equipment made him
determined that the new hospital he had designed and
which, by September, was well under way, would have all
it needed. In letter after letter to the Department of the
Interior in Washington, D.C., he requested everything he
would need. This was no time to be reticent, he reasoned.
He had noted the federal government touted the colony as
a working model and was eager to assure the nation that
the farm families had proper provisions.

As a result, Washington readily fulfilled his requests,
and Ohlson's railroad regularly deposited modern medical
paraphernalia at the Palmer station. The community was
impressed. "The doctor was very good at getting what he
wanted," Sherrod said. "No one seemed to be able to say
'No' to him."

Ground for the hospital was broken July 22, 1935, and
the building admitted its first patient on November 2. It
was christened Valley Hospital with proper ceremony.

"Oh, it was a wonderful advancement for the residents
of the valley," Sherrod recalled. And especially wonderful, he pointed out to the colony, was the electricity from
the new diesel generator. No more gasoline lanterns.

Albrecht, the staff, and the community had good reason

to be proud. When completed, the hospital would have separate wards for women, men, and obstetric patients; an operating room; laboratory; sterilization and x-ray rooms; doctor's office; dentist's office; waiting room; dining room; kitchen; boiler room; and cool storage under the kitchen.

"There was also a very nice nursery and delivery room," said Sherrod. This was a godsend for the lusty, young population that began turning out more than eighty babies a year.

Albrecht sometimes felt overrun by the parents, many of whom caused him more consternation than their ill children. Frequently they took up his office time trying to win his support in their neighborhood battles or for their endless complaints against the administration.

Mary Bagoy Lakshas, one of his nurses, says he was particularly effective in cooling off the more dissident colonists. "They would arrive for an appointment with their kids, full of anger and very demanding," she said. "The doctor was always kind and patient with them so that by the time they left they were smiling and everything was okay. They came to him for a lot more than medical treatment. They liked to dump their troubles on him and he understood that."

He also developed some tricks when parents interfered with his treatment, insisting on an alternative remedy and instant cure.

"Sometimes he'd prescribe a certain color aspirin for a child, like red ones," Sherrod said. "If the mother came back and said the red ones didn't work, then he'd pull out some green ones and tell her they'd be more effective. They were the same medication, of course, but the strategy worked every time."

Tonsillectomies were a popular procedure of the times, and with more than three hundred children in the settlement Albrecht did his share of them. But now he had another problem. As the settlers moved into new homes on their land parcels, Albrecht found his patients often lived miles from the hospital. This imposed particular difficulty with young patients since few parents had any transportation other than a horse.

"So I would go myself or send Max in the panel Dodge truck that was our ambulance to get through the mud and collect the children, usually about four or five of them, who were due for tonsillectomies the next day," Albrecht said. "The nurses would have a party for them with balloons, ice cream and food and get them ready for the next day.

"Children are not the easiest to give anesthesia to, particularly if it's ether," Albrecht said. "We used a drip method because that's the easiest to control, but the kids hated it. We'd tell them we were going to put a cone over their nose and then we'd say, 'You're going to smell something. If you don't like it, just blow it away.'

"And of course they'd try to blow it away and to do that meant taking a deep breath so before long they were anesthetized," he recalled with a laugh. After two nights in the hospital, the youngsters were given a ride back home in the truck-ambulance.

However, Albrecht found he needed a particular knack that was not in his black bag nor in his training. Although the federal government fulfilled his requests for equipment and supplies, it did nothing to provide for the hospital's operating budget. The hospital had to be self-supporting through patients' fees, not easily collected from the colonists.

How was he to keep the new hospital going? His government contract paid him $250 a month for tending to the colonists, but wisely he had installed a fee system for the area's homesteaders—$75 for delivery and prenatal care or for an appendectomy, for example. The fees were charged to patients' accounts and they paid the ARRC when they could. But given the burdens of the depression, it could take three or four years before the bills were settled.

"This didn't bring in any cash to pay my nurses, and I needed a minimum of five to cover me," Albrecht said. "It was even discussed—and thank heavens the colonists didn't know this—that the hospital would serve only for emergency care and other patients would be sent to Anchorage."

That idea delighted Colonel Ohlson, for it would bolster his own Anchorage Railroad Hospital. The success of the new Palmer facility, its modern equipment, its spacious design and the pride it inspired in its community caused the railroad manager much concern for the growth of his own hospital and no small amount of envy.

Ohlson could be a formidable opponent. His railroad was the lifeline of the area and his influence and power were unquestioned.

Furthermore, he was an imperious, indomitable sourdough who accepted defeat poorly. Albrecht, ever the peacemaker, had no wish to take him on and lose his friendship. But he also knew he must safeguard the life of Valley Hospital.

Even in the facility's brief existence, its reputation for quality care had extended well beyond colony borders. Now people in the growing town of Wasilla, ten miles north on the railroad line, turned to the Palmer hospital for care. It was a haven for miners and homesteaders in the area. Albrecht was even conducting examinations of school children throughout the valley and finding plenty of health problems. His hospital, he knew, was essential and, best of all, it was nearby.

Still, there was the unanswered question of how to meet its operating expenses. The colony management knew as well as he that the hard-pressed patients would not return enough in payments to underwrite nurses and other staff. To some at ARRC, use of Ohlson's hospital seemed a sensible solution.

Albrecht could keep his hospital at full strength, he realized unhappily, only by assuring the management he would find the necessary cash. This would require more innovation than the red and green aspirin tactic. Somehow, despite his demands as medical director and despite a feeble economy, the doctor now would have to make the grade as a fund-raiser.

# CHAPTER 3
# Seeking Solvency

*Dr. Albrecht stands outside the Palmer
colony's infectious disease ward.*

Alaska's glorious summer of 1935, with its fields of wildflowers and huge runs of salmon, gave the colonists no hint of what was to come. But in September, the wind off the glaciers sent an indisputable message that the mild weather was nearing its end. Soon, the harsh Alaska winter would begin its seven-month grip on the land.

To Albrecht, it seemed as if there had hardly been a summer. Running his makeshift hospital while trying to design a new one had left him few hours for the fishing he loved. Fishing, Albrecht believed, was the best part of summer. His friend, Manley Sweazey, also an ardent fisherman, understood the doctor's yearnings and devised a secret plan of action.

It was Sweazey's ploy to come to the back door of the hospital with a glint in his eye and announce urgently, "There's an emergency at Fish Creek!" This was all the signal Albrecht needed. Together the pair would head for the creek, famed for its salmon runs. A couple of hours on the stream never failed to restore Albrecht's belief he had come to his rightful place on earth.

Fishing was therapy for Albrecht. He loved to share the local waters with tourists, insisting afterward they taste some of Alaska's bounty. When a New York doctor, H. E. Kleinschmidt, passed through the colony, Albrecht saw his chance to enlighten an Easterner.

Kleinschmidt was thrilled to catch a rainbow trout or two. Later, he wrote his impressions to the editor of *The American Mercury*:

"Dr. Albrecht is doctor, hospital superintendent, health officer, and father confessor rolled into one. He runs one of the neatest little hospitals I've seen anywhere. He knows practically everybody, takes part in the joys and woes of the settlers, participates in the debates, leads the singing, boosts the fair.

"On one morning when I was there, Dr. Albrecht worked like a Trojan among his patients so that he might have the afternoon to take me and another doctor fishing. He drove like mad over thirty miles of godawful gravel roads, meantime keeping up a vivacious conversation.

"He fished with the same gusto that he put into his work that morning and into the feast of trout we enjoyed that evening by the side of the lake. On the way back he detoured to a lone shack to say hello to 'Old Doc,' a broken-down chiropractor whose only companion is a lean, rachitic hound.

"Next we slipped into a summer camp and scared the breath out of some twenty housewives who were enjoying a week's vacation there. They were singing good old Rotary songs which echoed across the silver lake. The surprised ladies fairly took Doc to their collective bosoms, for hadn't he delivered their babies and cared for their husbands and children?

"Then more miles of jolting in the old Lizzie. My buddy and I tumbled into bed after our strenuous day but not Doc. He sat up all night with a poor fellow who had fractured his skull, and gently closed his eyes about the time we yawned ourselves awake."

Just as Albrecht's affection for his newfound paradise deepened, most colonists, too, grew to appreciate their Alaska life. Some still clung to their waning celebrity status fostered by roving journalists who stopped by for a few days to record interviews and write stories that were usually slanted against the ARRC. But the need for normalcy, to establish roots, was as undeniable as the fresh snow on the mountain tops.

If the farmers required any convincing the party was over, it came with Washington's announcement in early fall, 1935, that farmers could no longer run up debts at the commissary. The Department of the Interior had tired of the cavalier way many squandered their federal stipends and then complained they were broke.

Early in October Lt. Col. Leroy P. Hunt, administrator of the colony, gathered the farm families together for some blunt words.

"The presents are all gone," he said. "The Christmas tree has been thrown out into the brush pile and from now on you must learn to live within your budgetary allowances. Get in, pull together in harmony and you will have the chance of a lifetime."

It was a statement that drew some grumbling but most

acknowledged they were ready to make the experimental colony work.

On October 11, 1935, the transient workers started heading back to California, having laid the foundation for the last house and begun work on the hospital interior. Within two weeks all of them would be gone, turning over final construction projects to Alaskan labor and taking their company physician, Dr. Earl E. Ostrum, with them. Albrecht's sense of isolation grew.

As the colonists moved into their new homes, often miles from the hospital, Albrecht tried to reduce his visiting hours. Travel over the deeply rutted dirt roads in the Dodge truck-ambulance was time-consuming and, in the winter, often dangerous. He always alerted the community garage when he set out on a house call with instructions to look for him if he was gone too long. More than once his vehicle was pulled from a ditch where it had slipped in the ice or mud.

"The farm families wanted to have their babies at home but I insisted they come to the hospital. Otherwise I could be sitting in some farm kitchen when I was needed at the hospital," Albrecht recalled. In his six-plus years at the Palmer hospital, he sent only one patient to Anchorage for a Caesarean delivery.

Although he resisted pleas for home deliveries, he did not hesitate to answer an emergency call from a farmer whose pregnant wife began bleeding profusely in her final term. The woman lived in Butte Camp, far from town on the Matanuska River, and Albrecht was able to drive the truck-ambulance only as far as the river's bridge, which could not bear the vehicle's weight. From there he hiked to the home where he found the woman needed immediate hospital care.

"All we could do was rig up a logging sled with a wagon and place the patient on a bed of straw and blankets,"

Albrecht said. "This was pulled by a Caterpillar tractor. I followed on horseback to the bridge where I turned over the horse to a farmer and took the woman to the hospital in the ambulance.

"The happy ending to this difficult experience was that in about three weeks the mother delivered a healthy infant and both mother and child were well," he says. But the incident increased his concern about staffing the hospital adequately.

"I've got to get someone here who can take over for me if necessary," the doctor told Max Sherrod. "Suppose we get a burst appendix here and I'm not around. Or I'm handling a skull fracture at the time. And even if I'm available I've got to have a trained operating room assistant. Which I don't have now."

"Why don't you ask the management for another doctor?" Sherrod suggested. "There's more than one hundred families here and you're even doing work with people outside the colony. That ought to be a pretty good argument for some more help."

The argument was not good enough for the federal government. Albrecht pleaded his case to the ARRC but the Department of the Interior in Washington, D.C., held to its premise that the hospital must finance its own administration. What, he wondered worriedly, did this mean for his duties as medical director?

With persistence—and Albrecht was becoming noted for his persistence—he was given another nurse, bringing the nursing staff to six, and that encouraged him. He still needed a trained operating room assistant, however. Injuries were common in the developing territory. The workers used construction equipment, the farmers cleared their land with machines and axes, the miners dug coal and gold from the nearby mountains, and all were at risk. And in the event of a casualty, they headed for his hospital.

Nurses were woefully scarce in Alaska in the 1930s and were often overworked to the point of exhaustion. The Bureau of Indian Affairs and the American Red Cross assigned these intrepid women to cover, alone, areas the size of a Lower 48 state. Travel frequently was by dog sled with a Native leading the way. When the nurse arrived at her destination, she was expected to treat all manner of illnesses and disabilities—from chicken pox to complicated births to heart attacks to broken limbs. A hospital assignment would have been a holiday for these saints but they could not be spared from the field.

Albrecht had, in his own home, a thoroughly capable operating room supervisor—his wife, Blanche. But Blanche declared she had put her nursing days behind her when she left Philadelphia. She slipped readily and firmly into the role of homemaker.

Not to be deterred, Albrecht reasoned that if he could not entice Blanche, then he would appeal to her assistant at Abington Memorial Hospital, Ruth Kelly, who also had solid operating room experience. And as he was to do many times in his career, he proved to be persuasive.

Blanche met Ruth at the train station when she arrived in Anchorage in December 1935 and showed her to her quarters in the new hospital, which was almost completed. Kelly thought the building was fine and the entire situation an exciting escapade.

"It was just great," she said. "I had a room right in the hospital and paid $25 a month for it and $25 a month for board. I earned $150 a month so I netted $100 a month, the most I had ever cleared. I even had a Coleman stove in my room."

Kelly had come just in time. One week after her arrival the colony suffered a sad loss when Evelyn Emberg's husband mistakenly poured aviation fuel into the family's kitchen range. Evelyn and her husband, George, and their three-year-old daughter, Dixie, escaped from the blaze, which demolished their home, but both mother and child were badly burned.

The mother died the following evening of shock and burns. Dixie, her face blackened, was unable to speak and in great pain from third-degree burns.

"I know it hurts, honey, but try to swallow some water," Albrecht whispered to the little girl. She looked steadily at him with lashless eyes and obediently opened her small mouth. Three days later, while the community was trying to raise money to send her to a plastic surgeon, Dixie died. Camp children carried her coffin to the tiny cemetery.

It was not Albrecht's first death at the colony—an Indian woman with a long record of lung disease had died of double pneumonia in November—but it deeply grieved him, reminding him of the dangers to children in this rough land.

"We saw all sorts of terrible things happen to youngsters," nurse Claire Kopperud recalled. "They had a tough time of it. The farmers had a way of clearing the land by cutting off trees about three feet from the ground. The stumps were pulled out by cables and drum winches with horses, and the stumps and trees were then heaped into piles and burned.

"It was not unusual for the fires to get out of control and to smolder underground for a long time. Children frequently tumbled into the smoldering undergrowth," she said. "Burns were sometimes so severe that the children were sent to hospitals Outside, usually to Chicago. I remember with sadness the suffering by many of these hapless youngsters. No one should ever think the colonists had it easy. It was a very hard life."

Peril seemed to be constant in Alaska. Albrecht was particularly concerned about the fate of miners. In an area rich in coal, gold, and other resources, safety often was sacrificed for production. That resulted in accidents.

When a miner was brought in with a compound fracture in December, the event had important repercussions for Albrecht. With the case, an idea formed in his mind, began to grow, and became such a compelling possibility he dared to hope it might solve the financial problems of his hospital.

"I looked at the fact that there were about six hundred men in the mines in the valley," Albrecht said. "And I knew that they were all subject to illness and accidents. But they didn't have doctors, of course, at the mines. We in Palmer were the closest.

"So I figured that I would offer to take care of the men for four dollars per man per month—I'd get one dollar, the hospital three dollars. Furthermore, I'd give pre-employment exams without charge to determine whether the man had a bad back or a hernia, syphilis, or an infectious disease. This way the bosses would know what they're getting. And this would give me the money to hire the five nurses I needed."

The proposal was cheered by the miners and their bosses. The prosperous Independence Mine and others readily signed contracts with the doctor. They offered an important inducement to workers in the hazardous occupation.

"The four dollars was to take care of compensible occupational injury and so on," Albrecht said. "It didn't cover pneumonia, appendicitis, and alcoholism, for example. And it built up my budget because I lost money on only one man who had a fractured femur and was laid up for six months.

"But in this way the men got acquainted with me so that if they ran into any health problems later they came to me for attention. And that became part of my private practice."

He was making medical history with the system. He had instituted a program of prepaid medicine, a concept that years later would become a national industry.

Albrecht was aware he would have to reach outside the colony for ways to fund the hospital, but opportunities were slim. He already cared for the fifty or so homesteaders in the area without seeing much profit. The only other residents were poor Indians who preferred their own medical practices.

"The Indian women thought that as long as they nursed their babies, they couldn't get pregnant," Claire Kopperud recalled. "It didn't work, of course, but still they would nurse them for years, along with any new infants. Dr. Albrecht was disgusted with the practice and concerned about these children, but couldn't get the mothers to change their ways.

"One day he came back from a visit to a village with a boy about four or five years of age and said, 'I want you to wean this child from his mother. There are two younger ones at home who are nursing as well.'

"The kid was like a little animal and strong. He scratched us into bleeding ribbons but we finally got him to eat enough food so he would have normal nourishment. We all said, 'Hooray!' when after about two weeks the kid could finally go home.

"But I'll never forget that the child was in a bed about six or eight feet from the door, and when his mother rounded the corner he bounded from the bed and pulled open her shirt front," Kopperud said, laughing. "So much for our two-week treatment."

The state of the Natives' health, and especially the children, was disturbing and frustrating to Albrecht. It was difficult to travel to the villages, and villagers did not always accept modern medicine readily. When a road between Anchorage and Palmer was completed in 1936, Albrecht saw an opportunity to make a change.

At Eklutna, an Athabaskan Indian village halfway between Palmer and Anchorage, the BIA had established a
school for Native teenagers from all over the territory who
showed intellectual promise. With the new road, Albrecht
now had an easy run to the school in the Dodge truck.
Flushed with the success of his medical contracts with the
mines, he offered a similar arrangement to George
Morelander, the principal, who promptly named Albrecht
medical director of the school.

"They had one public health nurse taking care of the
students—there were about 140 of them, all exceptional
kids—and right on my first visit I could see there was active tuberculosis among those children," Albrecht said.
"And here they were, living in dormitories. I couldn't believe it.

"I had had special training in TB while a senior medical student. In fact, I lived in a sanatorium run by Jefferson
Medical College and worked there, which gave me an income. Got my room and board that way. So I knew TB
when I saw it," he said.

"I asked the public health nurse for their chest x-rays.
'Don't have any,' she said. 'Don't have any?' I said. I was
appalled. 'Well, we've got to have them taken,' I said. 'We
can't have these children coughing around here and spreading TB among those who don't have it.'

"I talked the Alaska Tuberculosis Association into taking the x-rays," Albrecht said. "I couldn't get anyone in
Washington, D.C., to approve them, which was unbelievable. And I found twenty cases, including six with active
sputum. These, of course, are the ones who must be isolated.

"So I made a wing in the hospital, and it became an
isolated sanatorium. I would guess it was the first in
Alaska," Albrecht said. "This was in the days before drugs
and all we could give them was rest and good food. Usually

we collapsed their lungs, too. It was all we knew to do back then. The BIA paid us five dollars for each TB patient and that gave me some further financial security for my hospital."

He was a long way from solvency, however, and he knew it. Late in 1937 he decided to search for funds in the Lower 48, since he felt he had tapped what was available to him in Alaska. He announced he and his wife would be taking a three-month trip to the East and he was leaving a replacement physician, Dr. Kenneth Payson from Ketchikan, in his place.

Although the Albrechts visited friends and family along the way, there was a more serious purpose to the journey. Paying his own expenses, Albrecht traveled to the Kellogg Foundation in Michigan, the Friends Society in Philadelphia, and the Rockefeller Foundation in New York, asking for $10,000 to $15,000 just to hire a nurse. No success. Even though he had a friendly session with Nelson Rockefeller, he came away empty-handed.

In desperation he decided to make a pitch to the U.S. Department of Health. Washington, he was convinced, was where the dollars were. And at a most propitious moment, the legendary Albrecht luck kicked in. He was directed to the Labor Department's Children's Bureau. The medical director, Dr. Edwin Dailey, was married to Dr. Romig's granddaughter.

"That was a big plus going for me because he understood how things were in Alaska, how difficult the living was," Albrecht said. "But a more important factor was the bureau's interest at that time in demonstration projects involving children and families. And we could shape our facilities very easily around that."

The bureau wanted Albrecht to prove that in a rural community, deliveries were safer in a hospital than at home. He agreed and had the data to substantiate his position:

Only one crib death had occurred in his tenure at the colony, and there had been no childbirth deaths. He credited the exemplary statistics to his insistence on hospital deliveries.

It was autumn of 1938 before money from the Children's Bureau began coming in, and only after the ARRC agreed to four conditions: The colonists were to support the hospital with prompt payment of bills; noncolonists—the area's homesteaders—were to be encouraged to use the Palmer hospital rather than the Anchorage facility; the Palmer hospital must be made available to the Bureau of Indian Affairs (actually, it had always been open to Natives); and the colony must continue and expand its maternal and child-health programs.

The bureau delineated terms for prenatal care, hospital delivery, and postpartum care—all requiring extensive record-keeping—and outlining firm specifications for treatment. The additional work for the staff was taxing, but the compensation was the salvation of the hospital. The new federal contract was a heartening annual grant of $50,000.

The agreement gave Albrecht the nurses he needed and allowed him to plan for an assistant. There was even a valuable and unexpected ingredient in the bureau's package—a contraceptive clinic for the Palmer hospital. Palmer may have been the frontier, but now it could offer a service found then only in progressive communities of the Lower 48.

"We gave out birth-control advice along with diaphragms and jellies, which is what they used in those days, and made us among the first in the nation to do so," Albrecht recalled.

Parenting became a highly personal and wondrous matter for the Albrechts about that time. Their marriage having brought no children, Earl had put out the word among his medical connections that he and Blanche were interested in adoption. In June 1940, they received a call from a Washington, D.C., agency telling them a baby girl was available. Ecstatic, they left Alaska to meet their infant daughter. Baby Jane Elizabeth, three weeks old, crossed the nation by train in a wicker basket and was introduced to Palmer by her beaming parents.

The Albrechts had moved from their tent into a two-bedroom home adjacent to the hospital in February 1936, the last of the colony residents to acquire a frame house. With the arrival of the baby, the home seemed too small, and they began planning a larger house, to be made of logs, on land Albrecht had bought north of town in Bailey Heights.

Meanwhile, hospital funding continued to weigh on Albrecht's mind.

While the Children's Bureau contract was a boon to the Matanuska Valley, Albrecht's accomplishment did not sit well with some Alaska officials who chafed at his ability to acquire funding from the federal government, particularly when such funding was limited. In 1941 he received bad news from Dr. Wayne S. Ramsey, the territory's director of maternal and child health.

"There's a shortage of $20,000 in appropriations from the U.S. Department of Labor's Children's Bureau," Ramsey wrote. "We won't be able to fund your maternal health program for next year."

Albrecht's reply was terse and resolute.

"This is a most successful program here and we can't continue without financial aid from the Territorial Department of Health," he wrote. "I need at least $6,000-$7,000 for next year. The funds must be found."

Admitting the Palmer family program was "the most outstanding one in the territory," Ramsey dug deep and, after some delay, fulfilled Albrecht's request. It had been an unpleasantly tense confrontation, with critical maternal

and child health at stake, but Albrecht refused to lose such
an essential program.

"At last I had the security I sought," he said. "With the
contracts with the miners, the Eklutna School, and then
the Children's Bureau, the hospital was saved for Palmer."
What's more, the Children's Bureau allocation also allowed
for the much-needed assistant physician. Dr. LeRoy Flora
was added to the staff in April 1941 to give Albrecht some
overdue relief from the job.

By now, the doctor was deep into community activities
and reveling in it. He had his hand everywhere: coaching
the girls' basketball team, starting a summer recreation
program for young people, forming a tennis club, mediating problems of the colonists.

He waged a vigorous campaign to bring the valley its
own electrical power system, helping to form the Matanuska
Electric Association in 1940.

When he, Blanche, and Jane moved into their new log
home in the spring of 1941, it had the area's first residential generator. He was determined his neighbors also would
have electricity.

As secretary of the electric association, he fired off letters to the Rural Electrification Administration that resulted
in a loan in 1941. The following year, power came to 150
valley customers—including the Albrechts—on ninety-three
miles of lines.

Albrecht served on the board of the United Protestant
Church, participated in its construction plans, and organized its social events.

During the winters he involved nearly the entire colony
in Christmas programs that featured the chorus he had
founded as well as every amateur entertainer in town. The
community hall was always filled for the occasion and
Palmer residents exulted in recounting each act for days
afterward.

Music had long afforded Albrecht profound pleasure, and once he and Blanche had moved from the tent, they began holding musicales in their home on Sunday evenings. Sometimes these featured performances by talented colonists or by Albrecht himself on the trombone, and other times he played his favorite records, almost always including some Bach. On winter nights, as his guests left his house after an evening of music, he was thrilled to hear them humming their way home across the snow.

The Albrechts' new five-bedroom home was considered Palmer's showplace. At their previous property, Blanche had produced gardens that drew spectators, and now she had a far larger plot to cultivate. Relishing her home, she seldom took part in the colony doings that Earl enthusiastically joined.

Elsie Havens Blue, a hospital nurse, believes Blanche suffered from migraines. "Earl often explained his wife's absence by saying she had a headache and I think that in some ways he was just too energetic for her," she said. "He was full of vigor, always involved in some activity and usually initiating them. He seemed to be tireless, both at work and at play."

Yet Blanche was a consummate hostess and delighted in entertaining, which she did with innovation and much care. Although it was said her house was so spotless "you could eat off the floor," she nevertheless laughed when Jane, in her high chair, tossed food on her expensive carpet.

Her interior decorating, with furnishings shipped north from Philadelphia's prestigious Wanamaker's store, overwhelmed the farm wives. "Why," said one, "do you know she even had material to match the color of the knotty pine woodwork?"

Refinement had come to Palmer. But not tranquillity. Just a few miles north of Anchorage, an extensive army base, Fort Richardson, was undergoing feverish construction as the threat of war grew. Alaska's vulnerability to Japan's military buildup became more evident, although it had taken a long while for Congress to comprehend the danger to the territory. Like other communities in Alaska, Palmer was nervous.

Albrecht, who had joined the Medical Reserve Officers' Training Corps while in college, knew he was a sure bet to be called up. Letters from the army began arriving at his office regularly in 1940, inquiring about his draft status. As long as he was in charge of the hospital, he stood a fair chance of avoiding conscription. But now he had a capable replacement with his assistant, Dr. Flora, and Flora, who had had polio as a child, had a medical deferment.

Albrecht tracked Hitler's march across Europe, noted the expansion in Japan's war machine, and was not surprised when Mussolini joined the offensive. "Before long, America will be involved in the war," he told Blanche, "and I'll have to serve."

Might as well get ready for it as best I can, he thought, and signed up for military correspondence courses. His concentration was on administration, since he felt it would apply to a variety of roles the war might demand of him. Merely a wise precaution, it seemed at the time, but it was one that affected his entire future.

Even before the Japanese struck at Pearl Harbor on December 7, 1941, Albrecht had his orders. On December 1, he donned his captain's uniform, turned over supervision of the hospital to Flora and headed to "Fort Rich." At least I'm still in Alaska, he consoled himself.

# CHAPTER 4

# Donning a Uniform

*During the war, Col. Albrecht (third from left)
shared his passion for fishing with army friends.*

Captain Albrecht, arriving at the 183rd Station Hospital at Fort Richardson in Anchorage on December 1, 1941, found it difficult to believe he was still in Alaska. The strict military code, his austere residency on base, the turmoil of an army preparing for battle were starkly different from his family practice with its tonsillectomies and childbirths, from the weekly chorus rehearsals at church, and from the comfortable pace of the Palmer colony. He felt transported to another part of the world. He found it reassuring to glance out the window occasionally and note the Chugach Range was still in its usual place.

He chided himself to be thankful for achieving important goals before he left the colony. He had been able to
put Valley Hospital on solid financial footing. He had been
able to rescue it from the threat of demotion to an emergency status. He had put it on a sound management system, and he had found a doctor to take his place.

Albrecht even managed to entice a dentist to Palmer,
which took some doing. Tooth decay and other dental problems were prevalent, especially among the children. He
could leave his Palmer practice with peace of mind.

His military assignment, though, brought plenty of tension as Fort Richardson raced to meet the threat of a Japanese attack. Until war threatened, Alaska's only protection
was one small military station in Haines. Anthony J.
Dimond, the territory's sole, nonvoting congressional delegate, had tried for years without success to convince Washington, D.C., that Japan posed a danger to Alaska.

Gen. George C. Marshall, then army chief of staff, testified urgently before a congressional subcommittee in early
1940 in favor of construction of an air base in Alaska, but
the subcommittee did not include it in an appropriation
bill that passed in the House on April 4, 1940. When Hitler
invaded Holland, Belgium, and Luxembourg five days later
and moved toward France, Congress had a quick change
of heart. In May 1940, funds were appropriated to create
Fort Richardson and Elmendorf Field.

Other airfields, army posts, and naval bases were hastily started through much of Alaska, but when eight hundred enlisted men and officers arrived in Anchorage on
June 27, 1940, no barracks were ready. Instead, the soldiers pitched their khaki tents in fields near the city.

They moved into military housing one month later, just
in time to greet Gen. Simon Bolivar Buckner, Jr., who was
given the awesome charge of fortifying the frontier almost
overnight.

Buckner became head of the Alaska Defense Force, later to become the Alaska Defense Command.

Construction workers, zealously recruited by a frantic War Department offering high wages, flooded into Alaska to build the military outposts and to upgrade the railroad in preparation for the heavy wartime equipment and supplies it would carry. Completing the Elmendorf Field airstrip before the heavy winter snows had the highest priority. It was finished in November. That done, attention focused on the base hospital, which was completed in April 1941.

Anchorage was swept up in the construction boom. The town barely had enough accommodations for its own citizens, let alone for the transient laborers. Housing was so scarce many workers slept in parks. Bars obliged them by staying open all night, and prostitutes did a flourishing business.

The 183rd Station Hospital, however, was a model of military decorum. Working there was a respite for Albrecht. His six-year tenure as Palmer's only physician had exhausted him.

While there were no war casualties in the 250-bed hospital, seventy-eight hundred military personnel occupied the base in 1941, resulting in a steady supply of patients.

"I have been put in charge of what we call a 'dirty ward,'" he wrote his family in Pennsylvania. "That means it has infectious diseases and infected post-operative conditions, abscesses and other so-called unclean, infective patient diseases. And I like the work. We're on a regular schedule and I'm associated with fine physicians."

Albrecht looked forward to brief visits to Palmer, which he was allowed to make for two days every six weeks. Joyously, he would make his way through the town, greeting friends, catching up on news at the hospital with Dr. Flora. He would arrive with a huge bag of peanuts, and call on Louis Odsather, manager of the cooperative store. Odsather liked peanuts almost as much as Albrecht did, and the two of them laughed and reminisced as they worked their way through the bag. Stella Odsather, Louis' wife and the daughter of Don L. Irwin, the first ARRC manager, said, "They shelled those peanuts so fast their hands looked like a pair of little squirrels."

These visits home were pleasant reprieves from the fear of invasion that gripped Fort Richardson—and indeed the entire nation—on December 7, 1941. On his first Sunday at the fort, Albrecht had attended services at the Presbyterian Church, then joined a doctor friend for lunch in town. A radio was playing and soon announced the fateful news of the Pearl Harbor attack. Troops stationed at the fort were ordered to return there immediately. As Albrecht drove back, he heard the incessant ringing of the fort's bells.

"The entire area was put on blackout," Albrecht recalled, "but at the hospital, the windows had no shades. We couldn't leave our patients in the dark—after all, we had to attend to them—so all of us, doctors, nurses, everybody available, spent the night pasting black paper on the glass."

Albrecht and other medical officers were given pistols to wear on duty, underwent foxhole drills regularly, and were instructed how to protect the patients during an air raid.

"We were, in a sense, in a war zone," Albrecht said, "because they found Japanese ships cruising northward in the North Pacific and they were coming in the direction of Anchorage. The southern belly of Alaska was very open to attack."

Adding to the nervousness was the scarcity of fighter bombers and other war planes in Alaska. "I remember the day the first large bombers came into the Anchorage area," Albrecht said. "We were all out there cheering and waving because it was a welcome sign that we were getting defensive airplanes."

Although Alaska braced for invasion, it did not come until six months after Pearl Harbor, and then it was not on the vulnerable mainland but on the bleak Aleutian Islands. On June 3, 1942, enemy bombers and fighter planes raided Dutch Harbor. The following day, Japanese soldiers landed on the remote, sparsely populated islands of Kiska and Attu. After easily subduing the few Aleut inhabitants, the Japanese set about building permanent bases there.

By that time, Albrecht had become chief of surgery at the hospital. The previous February, he had been called into the colonel's office and told he would assume the position on March 1, 1942. It was not a post he coveted.

"Colonel, I'm very contented with my work on the wards and I'd be happy to remain there," he said.

"Albrecht, you're in the army now," he was told sharply. "You'll be chief of surgery March 1." Albrecht began to regret somewhat the many Army correspondence courses in administration he had taken that qualified him for the job.

While the Japanese occupied Kiska and Attu, Albrecht prepared for casualties certain to come when and if the United States sought to retake the two Aleutian islands, but it was nearly a year before an invasion was launched. On May 30,1943, under a joint force led by navy Adm. T. C. Kincaid, the Seventh Infantry Division of the Seventeenth Infantry from California, with the aid of the Eleventh Army Air Force, conquered the Japanese invaders in the grim battle of Chicagof Harbor on Attu.

The victory concluded nineteen days of bitter, hand-to-hand fighting. The combat cost the United States 432 lives and 110 wounded, but the greatest number of casualties— an additional twelve hundred—was due to adverse weather and terrain conditions and the scandalous fact that the soldiers had been unsuitably prepared and equipped. The California-based infantry, trained for battle in the African deserts, landed on Attu without any experience in arctic warfare and without proper clothing. As a result, many of the men lost their feet to frostbite.

The 183rd Station Hospital received most of the wounded and was ready for them. Shortly after Albrecht was made chief of surgery, the hospital added five hundred beds in new buildings scattered through the wooded foothills of the Chugach Range. The installation, known as Unit 2, was spread out seven miles from the main base and included barracks, airplane hangars, ammunition dumps, and other military facilities. Keeping in step with the Attu invasion plans, Albrecht had the surgeons of Unit 2 ready in May 1943 for what the war might demand.

"There was a constant threat for us to be invaded and bombed by Japan, which controlled the Pacific Ocean at that time," Albrecht said. "We were somewhat camouflaged so in case we were hit by bombs we would have only partial destruction in the dispersal area. Locating the new buildings from the main base offered some protection."

Two months after retaking Attu, on July 28, 1943, the United States went after the seventy-eight hundred Japanese believed to occupy Kiska, but the U.S. infantry found the foggy island deserted. Under low cloud cover and darkness, all had escaped on submarines. Still, the American campaign was tragic. Mines, booby traps, and especially "friendly fire" as scouts overreacted to forms and shadows in the fog, took twenty-one U.S. lives and wounded 121.

"Friendly fire" was a problem at Fort Richardson as well. "We had a lot of young troops just in the service for training purposes," Albrecht recalled. "Sometimes we had live ammunition in the training fields, land mines, and personnel mines. I never saw the need to have live ammunition." The situation was filled with grave risk. Albrecht remembers with sorrow one of his last surgical procedures. He and an associate surgeon amputated the feet of a soldier who had stepped on a land mine in training practice.

With the ending of the Attu-Kiska campaign, the prospect of battle casualties faded. However, there were more than bodies to be tended and healed. Elmendorf pilots were assigned to bomb the northern Kurile Islands of Japan, "a very hazardous mission," Albrecht said, "because they had no equipment or instruction to guide them there or to return safely. We'd send out about ten P-38 bombers and maybe six or even three would come back."

The high percentage of loss severely affected the morale of the young fliers, who sought out Albrecht and other physicians for psychological relief. "It was very difficult to work with them, to try to help them deal with that, but it was also part of our responsibility as doctors," he said.

An increasing number of such cases caused Albrecht to add Quonset huts to Unit 2 for the care of psychiatric patients. He insisted the wards be painted in cheerful, bright colors, free of bars or gates. Patients were given some freedom and daily routines.

Early in 1944, a new promotion took him away from the clinical work and surgery he relished. He was made executive officer of the hospital with the rank of lieutenant colonel and given a desk, mounds of paperwork, and responsibility for six other army hospitals—in Kotzebue, Barrow, Dillingham, Bethel, Skagway, and Nome. He was obliged to inspect these outposts, flying military planes in all sorts of weather. At last, wearing not a white coat but an army uniform, Albrecht reached Bethel.

The next spring, he was promoted to commanding officer at the hospital. He had heard the enlisted men and women assigned to the dispersal compound in the mountain foothills were unhappy to be away from the main base, and he had a remedy in mind.

It was similar to his remedy in Palmer when the farming families, far from their midwestern homes, suffered feelings of isolation and homesickness. There, Albrecht had formed choruses, staged live entertainment, and organized social events—anything to bring people together in a pleasant, friendly setting and improve morale.

The people at Fort Richardson were no different, he felt. They needed diversions. He convinced his superior officer, Gen. Richard E. Mittelsteadt, that the answer was a Red Cross building that would include a gymnasium, ice-skating rink, and activity rooms. Clubs for enlisted men and officers also were built. Albrecht carried the whole idea further by recruiting movie stars, sports figures, and other celebrities to visit the base and perform for the troops. Visitors included actresses Ingrid Bergman and Olivia deHaviland, boxer Joe Louis, comedian-entertainer Bob Hope and his wife Dolores, and violinist Yehudi Menuhin.

Meanwhile, the Albrechts had entered a cozy social circle in Anchorage. Among their friends were Bob Atwood, publisher of the *Anchorage Daily Times*, and his energetic wife, Evangeline; Herb Hilscher, a prominent public relations specialist and his wife, Miriam; city and military officials, and even Ernest Gruening, governor of the territory, and his wife, Dorothy.

The forty-mile drive from Anchorage, Albrecht's army duties, and gas rationing all curtailed their partying, but the Albrechts had another special reason for staying home nights. In May 1944, while on official business in Washington, D.C., Albrecht received a call from the same agency that brought little Jane into his life. This time there was a boy, nine days old, available for adoption. Was the colonel interested?

Albrecht was elated. "Of course!" he exclaimed. "I'll be

right over to get him as soon as I can make arrangements."

It was an optimistic statement from someone on active military duty in wartime, but Albrecht was not about to let regulations deter him. He needed help, he realized, and Blanche was too far away to provide it. But his sister-in-law lived within reach in Pennsylvania. Maybe she could come to his aid.

She could. Violet Albrecht, his brother Charles' wife, rushed to Washington. Together she and Earl collected the infant, already given the name of John Richard, and brought him to Bethlehem, Pennsylvania, to introduce him to Earl's mother. While the doctor finished his business in Washington, Violet cared for John.

Then Albrecht was on his own to get the baby home to Palmer. First, he sent off a telegram to his old fishing buddy, Manley Sweazey, now living in Seattle, proudly telling him of his new son. "Will call when in your town," Albrecht promised.

Toting bottles, diapers, and a supply of baby formula, Albrecht boarded a plane in Philadelphia with John snug in a basket. The plane's crew beamed over the baby and immediately named him "Little GI Joe." Some hustled to make up formula and sterilize bottles. Newspaper wire services picked up the story of the traveling pair.

The message to Sweazey turned out to be providential. When Albrecht arrived at the airport in Seattle, unexpected orders awaited him: He was to go to the army hospital in Portland, Oregon, and facilitate the discharge of some of his patients sent there from Fort Richardson. The temporary duty would take two weeks.

Albrecht looked at Little GI Joe, asleep in his basket, and wondered what to do with him. There was a sense he was breaking rules with his precious cargo. He could hardly expect the Portland hospital to set up a nursery for him.

Sweazey came to the rescue. He and his wife, Polly,

were delighted to care for John, now being called Jack. Two weeks later, Albrecht returned to Seattle, picked up the baby, and looked for a fast ride back to Anchorage. He found it at the military airfield.

"We've got a plane here assigned to a Fort Rich general, sir, and we have to get it back up there," a corporal told him. "Why don't you and the baby ride it up? No one has to know about it."

There was a moment of consternation when it was discovered the baby did not have the necessary papers to enter Alaska, whose territorial status in wartime set it apart from the rest of the country. But an enterprising noncommissioned officer decided the problem could be solved by listing the baby as "excess baggage."

Albrecht arrived at Fort Richardson in a state of excitement, anxious to get to Palmer and introduce Jack to his new family. But as he rushed through the terminal waiting room he was met by the general who stared at the basket with its blanketed contents.

"What have you got there, Albrecht?" the general demanded. "It's a baby, sir," Albrecht answered, not breaking his stride.

"A baby?" barked the general. "Where'd that baby come from?"

"Oh, you know where babies come from, General," Albrecht replied, flashing his brightest smile and heading for the door. He was out of the building and into the Alaska night air before the general could pursue the conversation.

In June 1944, with the threat of invasion by Japan remote, Albrecht closed the military hospital and consolidated medical care in the Unit 2 dispersal hospital. His patients now were often troops transferred from smaller hospitals or those being evacuated to the Lower 48. Much of the time he was off the base, inspecting the six military hospitals under his command and appraising the health of nearby communities.

"At no time was it allowable for me to treat civilians, but that didn't mean I couldn't talk to doctors about their work," Albrecht said. Increasingly, he realized tuberculosis was spreading within the Native population. It sorely troubled him. He had found cases of the dreadful disease among the Fort Richardson troops, but those he was able to treat.

As he had seen the war coming, Albrecht could see the war ending. With war over, Alaska's military hospitals could be available for wider uses. The prospect excited him. What an answer these institutions could be for treating the territory's TB patients! What those patients needed, he knew, was isolation, beds, nursing care—all in short supply.

He began writing letters to the Department of the Interior and the War Department, urging that thought and planning be given to turning over the military hospitals to the territory for TB sanatoriums. While on duty he also attended conferences in Juneau on Alaska's health problems, and made his concerns known.

When traveling to Washington, D.C., on military affairs, as he frequently did, he sometimes stopped in Juneau to talk about the TB problem with Col. George Hays, on loan to Alaska from the U.S. Public Health Service and serving as executive officer of the Territorial Board of Health. He had misgivings about Hays, which he expressed to Governor Gruening, saying that Hays had "annoyed and aggravated the military no end" and "his handling in public health matters in Alaska have not been too healthy." He warned Gruening to "guard against any increased power for him" and said any advancement "would be unwise."

However, he knew any effort to reduce tuberculosis in Alaska would have to involve Hays' office. Hays saw the foresight of staking first claims on the hospitals and supplied Albrecht with a list of important people to contact in Washington. Albrecht, never hesitant when it came to promoting a cause, reached them all plus a few other contacts of his own.

"In no way will I compromise any military connection," he told Hays, "but when I'm in Washington I will try to discuss the matter with whatever interested officials I can find." At such times he itched to be free of his administrative restrictions and back into a well-run hospital.

Administration, however, was the direction opening up for Albrecht during the spring of 1945. In March, Gruening wrote him a carefully phrased letter noting the legislature finally had passed a bill creating a comprehensive Department of Health that would give Alaska its first full-time commissioner. Did Albrecht know anyone fit for the job? Could Albrecht be released from the army in the event he himself was interested?

Albrecht suspected this was a firmer offer than the governor's casual tone indicated. In his years at Fort Richardson, he and Gruening had developed a friendship based on reciprocal respect. Gruening, a graduate of Harvard Medical School, was also a physician, although he never practiced medicine, preferring newspaper work and politics. But he spoke Albrecht's medical language and shared his concerns about health care for Alaskans.

The prospect was both enticing and troubling. Albrecht savored the thought of returning to his efficient, friendly Palmer hospital, to the interaction with patients, to the community he had come to love and to watching his children grow up in it.

During the war, the Albrechts had taken in a twelve-year-old girl, Virginia, from the Jesse Lee Home, a Seward orphanage operated by the Methodist Church. When the territory trembled in anticipation of a Japanese invasion, the home had issued a plea for Alaskans to house the children for the duration of the war. The Albrechts now had three children, and he ached to be with them. Although the war was ending, Virginia would continue to stay with them.

Still, the opportunities Gruening offered were galvanizing. Albrecht had seen enough of Alaska to know that its people, especially its Native population, desperately needed decent health care. Tuberculosis, disease, accidents, abysmal sanitation, a shortage of doctors and nurses, and inadequate medical facilities inflicted a heavy toll on the villages. The two men discussed the matter in private.

"Governor, let's be honest." Albrecht said. "I don't know anything about public health. I'm trained in preventive medicine."

"I don't know anything about it, either," said Gruening. "We'll learn together."

"Well, I'm pleased that you think of me in connection with this position," Albrecht said, "but I want you to know that I am not at all interested in any kind of politics. I must be able to be my own man."

Actually, at the time, Albrecht was involved in a political situation that had him fuming. Colonel Hays, whom the doctor distrusted, had denounced Dorothy K. Whitney, the supervisory nurse in the Territorial Department of Health branch office in Anchorage. Hays had charged her with "disloyalty, misconduct and insubordination," and had removed her from office. The details of the case were never made public.

The firing was too much for Albrecht, who had known Whitney for nearly seven years, including time in Palmer where she was a public health nurse. He regarded her with both affection and high esteem. When she asked him for advice, Albrecht showed he could throw a political punch or two.

Writing to Col. Edgar W. Norris, medical director of the
U.S. Public Health Service in Juneau, Albrecht demanded
Whitney not only be reinstated to her former position but
the entire matter be expunged from her record and all ac-
cusations withdrawn. Furthermore, he wanted Hays out
of office.

Although he had no authority to intervene, the doctor
prevailed. Whitney got her job back, her record was cleaned,
and Colonel Hays soon saw the wisdom of retirement.
Albrecht's only comment on the episode, when asked about
it later, was, "It reflected Hays' temperament. Dorothy was
an extremely competent nurse."

Despite the controversy, Hays, before he left Juneau,
wrote a brief memo to Gruening recommending Albrecht
for the position of commissioner.

The governor could not appoint the new commissioner—that duty belonged to the new Board of Health—
but he did appoint the board. Gruening was determined to
have Albrecht in his cabinet, and made his board selec-
tions with this very much in mind.

Rather than trying to sell Albrecht the individual to the
board, Gruening instead sold the position. He defined the
requirements in such a way—Alaskan experience, community practice, demonstrated administrative skills—that only
one person in the territory could fit the bill. By June 1945,
Albrecht was the board's unanimous choice. The position
would pay $8,400 for the first year with annual raises to
take it to $10,000, as fixed by law, at the end of three years.

For his part, Albrecht was required to request discharge
from the army. He was more than willing to do so; he had
been informed his next assignment, at age forty, would be
to Adak—a desolate outpost in the Aleutians that he knew
all too well. The Juneau opportunity was looking better all
the time.

Now he had to turn to his Creator for guidance. An

integral part of Albrecht's life, prayer always supplied answers for him. In this matter, it had the blessing of numbers: He would be able to provide good health care for far
more people as a commissioner than as a physician in
Palmer. It was a convincing reality.

Taking the health department position would mean sac-
rifices of time and family, unsparing pressure and undoubtedly the hardest work he would ever do. "But I have always listened to my Lord and I could not deny the call,"
he says.

With a flush of optimism and a heady sense of venture, he wrote the Board of Health a letter of acceptance.
But in anticipation of an eventual return to Palmer, he and
Blanche decided to rent—not sell—their handsome log
home.

# CHAPTER 5
# Family Roots

*Earl (center rear), parents Charles and Elizabeth, and brother Charles Jr. posed for this family portrait in 1912.*

Awave of nostalgia overtook Lieutenant Colonel Albrecht as he cleaned out his desk in the 183rd Station Hospital in June 1945. The army had been good to him, and he had gained priceless knowledge and extraordinary experience in his assignments. He had reaped an insight into Alaska from Ketchikan to Barrow, more authority and responsibility than he had ever had. And he had relished it.

That he had done well was clearly recognized, from the lowest foot soldier to the commander. As word of his retirement filtered through the base, many stopped by his office to offer best wishes and thank him for his help. Plaudits came pouring in from those who had worked with him.

Capt. Frederic Witmer, hospital chaplain, praised him for his "matchless Christian spirit and personality" and complimented him for "never lowering yourself in personal and social speech and conduct to win people" and for his "unfailingly fair and charitable treatment of all men."

Brig. Gen. Richard E. Mittelsteadt, commander of Fort Richardson, added his own tributes in a letter to Albrecht that extolled his "professional knowledge, keen and intuitive executive ability.

"The high morale and discipline in troops under your command are evidence of superior qualities of leadership," the general wrote as he awarded Albrecht a commendation for superior performance of duty. Then he ordered a full-dress parade for the departing doctor, an unheard-of honor for a lieutenant colonel. Albrecht had to muster all the control he could to hide the proud tears welling in his eyes as the troops saluted him while passing in review.

Albrecht's affection for the military once would have distressed his Moravian forefathers. Moravians formerly were so opposed to combat they were exempt from fighting in early U.S. wars. They took no sides during the American Revolution; instead, they tended the wounds of both the British and the Yankees in their hospital at Bethlehem, Pennsylvania, not far from Valley Forge and other battlefields. During the Civil War, Moravian families were torn apart as sons sought to fight for the Union cause against the tenets of their peace-loving parents.

Listening after dinner as his father, a Moravian clergyman, read from the Bible and Moravian texts, young Albrecht learned his forebears had come to America from Germany in the late 1730s for the sole purpose of bringing knowledge of Jesus Christ to the Indians. This they would do through their exceptional powers of healing, not asking for commitment but trusting in the example of their faith to inspire conversion. A germ of purpose began to grow in his mind.

Albrecht's father, Charles, was born in the Germanic community of Jefferson County, Wisconsin, and could speak both English and German. His mother, Elizabeth, grew up in Pennsylvania. After Albrecht's parents married in 1904, they settled in Bruederheim, Alberta, Canada, where Charles was pastor of a Moravian mission and where their first child was born June 25, 1905, and christened Conrad Earl.

German was the language of Bruederheim. Elizabeth Albrecht, who spoke no German, felt stranded, able to converse only with her husband. Charles tried to lighten her spirits by hitching up their horse, Flossie, to a sled and giving Elizabeth a ride over the snow. Baby Earl went along, wrapped in a fur bunting and lying warmly at his mother's feet, out of the cold wind. When a young English-speaking girl arrived in the town one Christmas, Elizabeth wept with joy. Eventually, she, like Earl, learned to speak and write German.

But another means of communication among the Bruederheim Moravians eclipsed the language barrier, and that was their love of music. They particularly enjoyed the music of Johann Sebastian Bach, but they also appreciated all serious choral and instrumental works. Every Moravian child could either sing or play an instrument with competence. Earl Albrecht was given a trombone at an early age and he played it most of his life. He also had a fine "boy soprano" voice that matured into a creditable baritone. Music—its solace, exaltation, stimulation—became his constant companion.

Two other children, Charles and Gertrude, were born to the Albrechts.

The family followed the father's ministry from Bruederheim, where Earl attended a one-room school un-

til he was seven, to Canaan, North Dakota, where he gradu-
ated from Casselton High School.

These were farming communities, and afternoons and
weekends during his school years Earl put in long hours
helping with the corn and wheat crops. But he was not
interested in being a farmer, nor did his parents see that as
his future. The family assumed he would become an ordained Moravian minister. He saw no reason to disagree.

Even as a youngster he had given his parents encouraging signs he would continue in the clergy tradition. He
was the one other Bruederheim children called upon to
conduct burial services for their deceased pets, and he did
it with such reverence it seemed certain the animals were
headed for heaven.

Earl and his brother, Charles, played often in
Bruederheim with Florence Semper, whose father was also
a Moravian minister. The three had full run of the church.
One day they decided to have a wedding. Florence was
the clear choice to be the bride but Charles raised the question of who would be the groom.

"I will be the groom," Earl said with finality.

"Then I will be the preacher," Charles said.

"No, I will also be the preacher," announced Earl, not
willing to relinquish any authority.

"Then what will I be?" wailed Charles.

"You," said his brother, "will be the people." Earl had
quickly realized he could not be a very effective preacher
without a congregation.

Moravian youths who chose the ministry were headed
for an education at what was then Moravian College and
Theological Seminary in Bethlehem, Pennsylvania. The
school was Earl's father's alma mater, and Charles would
follow his brother there as well.

By the time Earl arrived on the campus in 1922 he had
decided not to use his first name, Conrad, because he "liked

the sound of Earl better." His classmates, however, called him "Duke," in recognition of his courtly ways.

Earl felt immediately at home at the college, loving its small size and intimacy. Furthermore, there was so much to do—basketball and baseball teams, glee club and band, dramatic productions. He joined them all.

The provincial city of Bethlehem, bounded on one side of the Lehigh River by the mammoth, steam-belching Bethlehem Steel plant and on the other by the genteel Moravian community, charmed him. Within weeks after arriving on campus, he was enrolled in the community's renowned Bach Choir and was a faithful baritone during his college years.

Summers he returned to North Dakota to work on the farms. "The vast open prairies were an inspiration to me," he said. "Just why I don't know. But the mile-long furrows without a bend, the wheat fields that took twelve hours or longer to go around, the vastness of the warm summer sky made an impression on me that to this day is vivid and real."

He surprised himself and his family by becoming business manager of the college newspaper and class yearbook. His classmates liked and respected him, twice electing him president.

It was an early indication Earl would never settle for life on the sidelines. He wanted a role in the action and not as just a team player; he insisted on being a leader. Some considered this to be obstinate, autocratic behavior; others saw it as confidence, optimism, ambition.

*Revista*, the college yearbook, said in one of its editions, "We have discovered [Earl] was misdirected energy personified. He needs only to be shown in what direction his energy can be applied." That was to be one of the hallmarks of his career; once set on a course, he ventured forth under a full head of steam.

Albrecht was, to all appearances, set on a course as he entered the theological seminary after his graduation from college in 1926. He was due to spend the next two years preparing for ordination and a vocation in the pulpit. But privately he was becoming painfully aware that his deep-rooted intentions to be an ordained minister were out of step with his true bent. "I simply felt unready for the ministry," he recalled. "I felt I was an unfinished person."

Also, he had been listening to Moravian doctors back from such places as Tibet, Nicaragua, and Alaska. An important date on Moravian students' calendars was the annual mission festival in the spring, when alumni, among others, came looking for eager recruits to hire. Albrecht had heard the medical missionaries' appeals to the students' humanitarian instincts and their heady tales of saving lives in exotic locales. The accounts claimed his rapt attention.

At the mission festival in his first seminary year, Albrecht circled the tables with their enticing displays and was intrigued by what he saw. He stopped at the exhibit on Tibet and gazed at the photographs of magnificent mountain scenery, happy native families, the proud Moravian doctor standing before a small but neat clinic.

He bent closer to study the pictures. "Think you'd like Tibet?" said a voice at his ear. Albrecht straightened and found a smiling doctor at his side. "If you'd like Tibet, look at this," the doctor said, holding out pictures of Alaska.

Albrecht had met up with Dr. Joseph Romig, who was the sole physician for the huge Yukon-Kuskokwim region in Western Alaska.

Romig, too, had a collection of photos featuring spectacular scenery, Native families, and his own small but neat clinic. He desperately needed help and had traveled all the way from Bethel, Alaska, where a Moravian mission was based, to persuade a seminary student or two to express their ministry in Bush medicine.

Albrecht listened attentively to Romig's tale of doctor-
ing in Alaska, its hardships and rewards. He glanced again
at the photo of the Tibetan clinic. It seemed to him he had
found his future.

For weeks he thought about the encounter with Romig,
the lure of Tibet, the life of a medical missionary. He sought
the opinions of his classmates, the guidance of his professors. And he turned to prayer. As the term ended, he had
made his decision to forego ordination and instead study
medicine as his way of serving his Lord.

But his father had to be reckoned with. First-born sons
of Moravian pastors were expected to continue the voca-
tional tradition. Albrecht headed home to spend the summer in North Dakota, where he would explain his change
of plans and pray his family would understand and accept
his decision.

Prayer is what it took. His parents listened solemnly as
Albrecht announced his intent to go to medical school. Then
father and son adjourned to an upstairs bedroom to ask
direction from God. When they had finished, the Rev.
Albrecht rose from his knees, clasped his son, and gave
him his blessing.

Four years at Jefferson Medical College in Philadelphia
were an unexpected expense, coming just as the nation
sank deep into the Great Depression. Albrecht hustled to
find part-time jobs, worked summers in Jefferson's tuberculosis sanatorium, and joined the Medical Reserve Officers Training Corps to earn money. Financing his tuition
was a ceaseless occupation during his medical studies.

Early in his first year at Jefferson he learned he would
not be going to Tibet, his first choice. The Moravian Church
had divided its missionary work so that the European
branch took over work in Asia and the U.S. branch got
responsibility for Nicaragua and Alaska. Recalling Romig,
he immediately substituted Alaska in his plans and, as he
thought about it, liked the prospect better.

Romig was no longer in Bethel but now was the medical director of the Anchorage Railroad Hospital. No matter, Albrecht thought. Western Alaska will only need me all the more, he told himself. And he set about arranging his courses so he would arrive there with the skills and knowledge to meet whatever the Bush would require of him.

Free time was a rarity for Albrecht during his Jefferson years; money was even scarcer. He had come to Philadelphia carrying a set of golf clubs that stood unused in his room because he could not afford the greens fees, even on public courses. One indulgence he allowed himself was to take the train to New York City and buy "standee" tickets for the opera and ballet. As always, music satisfied his needs.

Summers he spent fulfilling his ROTC obligations at Fort Snelling in Minnesota and working in Philadelphia. Travel home for Christmas vacations was too expensive. He celebrated instead by attending church and savoring the boxes of homemade cookies and candy his mother sent him. His only other travel was the short distance to Washington, D.C., knocking on the doors of the Bureau of Indian Affairs and of Alaska's representative, Anthony Dimond, pleading for assignment to Bethel.

The summer following his junior year at Jefferson, however, he felt a pull to visit his family, then living in Waconia, Minnesota. He skimmed the railroad fare from his savings and sent his parents the happy news that he was on his way, but would stop en route to visit a college friend.

Albrecht had made it halfway home when he was handed a telegram at a railroad stop. "Proceed home without delay. Father not well," it said. The visit with his college friend now canceled, Albrecht stayed on the train and two railroad stops later was handed another telegram. This one read, "Father has died."

Albrecht had used his time on the train to compose a

sermon he hoped to give at his father's church. It came in handy. He took his father's place in the pulpit for much of that summer as his mother prepared to move back to Bethlehem where she had friends and family. Then he was back for his final year at Jefferson.

The following June 1932, Albrecht's mother and sister attended his graduation, arriving in a chauffeur-driven car rented by Mrs. Albrecht's uncle, Dr. William Rentzheimer. Dr. Rentzheimer lived in Hellertown, adjacent to Bethlehem, and Albrecht made it a point to visit him and get encouragement when he was in the area. The doctor was elderly and in poor health but he was determined to see his great-nephew get his M.D.

"It was an exciting occasion for us all," Gertrude Albrecht Teufer, Earl's sister, remembers, "especially to have a chauffeur. But the best of it was Earl winning the First Surgery Prize, a beautiful gold medallion. Earl hadn't expected it, and we certainly didn't expect it, so it was a special surprise." He also got his bars as a first lieutenant in the army reserve.

Now postgraduate work beckoned. Albrecht took his at Abington Memorial Hospital in Abington, Pennsylvania, just outside Philadelphia. He would stay three years.

"We didn't have formal surgical residency in those days but, in fact, it was even better because I learned general surgery," Albrecht said. "I was an intern in residency training and surgery and also in pathology. I took a lot of pathology and gastroenterology at that time, which was very useful. Because I was going to Alaska, I was blessed by greater interest from the surgeons and the internists."

The attention came not just because of his plans. Albrecht had impressively demonstrated his skills and dedication and, despite his young age, was named chief resident physician and surgeon at Abington. There, he met and began dating Blanche Smith, supervisor of the operating room.

As he gained medical experience, Albrecht felt his crusade to go to Bethel deserved some new respect so he returned again and again to the BIA and to Representative Dimond. But the answer was always the same: When the BIA builds a hospital there you will be assigned to it. He was becoming increasingly irritated by the reply and despairing of his future in Alaska until he received a call in June 1935, from Dr. Romig.

"Earl, we have an opening at the railroad hospital here in Anchorage," Romig said. "Are you interested?"

"Well, doctor, you know I really want to go to Bethel," Albrecht hedged.

"Oh, you'll get there eventually, but we need you here," Romig insisted. "And we need you right away. There's just two of us—me and Dr. Walkowski—and the place is growing. What do you say?"

Although he could feel excitement rising, Albrecht decided to be cautious. "Let me think about it," he said.

The next weekend, Albrecht made a trip to Bethlehem to discuss the proposal with his mother, bringing Blanche with him. Mrs. Albrecht was convinced her son should grasp the opportunity. She was relieved when she learned he and Blanche planned to marry. One could not be certain, after all, about Alaskan women!

"None of us was surprised that Earl might go to Alaska," his sister Gertrude said. "We always knew he had his heart set on the place." When Albrecht returned to Philadelphia, he called Romig with the news that he would be honored to join his team in Anchorage.

Boarding a boat at Seattle for Seward in 1935, the doctor eagerly looked northward to Anchorage and his assignment as the lowest-ranking doctor at the Railroad Hospital. In 1945—a decade later almost to the day—he headed for Juneau as the territory's first full-time commissioner of health and would have all Alaskans in his care.

# CHAPTER 6
# TB Battle Begins

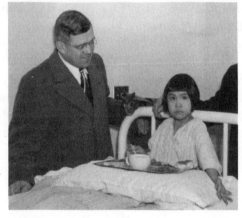

*Health Commissioner Albrecht sees a young TB patient in Sitka's Mount Edgecumbe sanatorium.*

J uneau had never appealed to Albrecht. The former farm boy had too much country in him to cotton to the insu lar coastal city. He loved the soft air of the Matanuska Valley, so different from the pungent sea breezes off Gastineau Channel. With no roads out of the city, he felt trapped by Juneau's steep, encircling mountains that limited traveling to boat and plane. His spirit basked instead in the sunny fields of Palmer, in the hospital he had designed, in the friendships he had made in the valley and in Anchorage.

Still more unpalatable to him was the capital's political

tension, even when the legislature was not in session. There was a saying about the town that "politics are served hot with every meal." It was a merciless, competitive environment with each elected representative determined to grab the most for his constituency without concern for principles. Albrecht worried that he and his department would be shackled by such a dishonest policy.

Then there was the weather. "It rains all the time there," he complained to Blanche. "And if it isn't rain, it's mist and fog." So his enthusiasm was almost as damp as the slopes of Mount Juneau as he headed to Southeast Alaska.

Public health care of Alaskans was regulated at that time by a board comprised of one member from each of the four judicial districts and the governor. A physician headed the board part-time as commissioner, with the post circulating among Juneau doctors. The needs of Natives were met by the Bureau of Indian Affairs, which operated hospitals—usually understaffed—in seven Bush communities. The BIA also provided a coterie of overworked, itinerant nurses and seventeen nursing centers. Episcopal and Roman Catholic missions had set up hospitals in the Interior and along the western coast, but these were limited in their services.

Shortly after the announcement of his appointment on July 1, 1945, Albrecht settled into an office in the cramped, musty building that housed the department in downtown Juneau. He eyed the agency's organization with misgivings. The divisions were largely separate fiefdoms, he realized, with little coordination. Public health nursing, sanitation engineering, infectious disease control, and other sections were autonomous bodies. And although he did not dispute their diligence and commitment, the staff was not only leaderless but hopelessly insufficient.

Within days after arriving, he carried his concerns to Gruening. Over the years, Albrecht and the governor had developed a mutual affinity that began effortlessly and, with time, intensified. Their conversations, in the governor's mansion and in his private office, ranged far beyond their shared medical interests, with Gruening often seeking Albrecht's views on such matters as the evil of fish traps and the unfairness of high freight rates.

"I never could understand why I was consulted by him in many matters far removed from medicine," Albrecht said. "I attributed it to the fact that I was a fellow physician that gave us this close relationship."

Gruening had plans for his new health commissioner. Albrecht, the governor saw, was not only proficient as an administrator but also had an inspired, even impassioned determination to achieve goals. Time after time, he persisted, usually alone, to win his way. Opposition and disappointment did not discourage him. Never offensive, always solidly informed, he pleaded his cases with a benevolence that left his listeners believing they had just heard a powerful sermon.

In their professional association, Gruening, the master statesman, instructed Albrecht in building on that talent.

"He taught me how to do things as a cabinet member, how to be persuasive," Albrecht said. "He was a man who was a missionary. He had a love and a compulsion to help people, and a zeal that was evident in his work. He was a hard master, a driver, a politician and knew how to exploit a political situation. I will always respect him."

Now, as Albrecht outlined the inadequacies of his department, Gruening countered with a challenge. The two frequently shared their fears about the inroads of tuberculosis, particularly among the Native population, and the governor agreed the problem must be faced. He would not allow flaws in the health department to impede the effort.

"Earl, you have to go out and tell the people of Alaska how bad tuberculosis really is," Gruening said.

"They know it already," Albrecht answered glumly.

"But they have to be impressed, so impressed that they

will write letters to me about it," Gruening continued. "I've got to have a stack of letters from them demanding some action."

"For what reason?" Albrecht asked.

"So I can call a special session of the legislature and we can get an appropriation that will not only straighten out your department but will eradicate tuberculosis from this territory," the governor answered.

It was a mandate Albrecht welcomed. He was skeptical whether letters would sway the legislature, but politics was the governor's business. For himself, he was curious to know the true extent of the disease in the territory. Alaska Native Service, a federal agency providing health services, estimated between 3 percent and 27 percent of the Bush villagers were infected, but that did not include the rate in the non-Native community or in the cities. Albrecht feared the infection rate was greater than anyone knew.

The history of tuberculosis in Alaska is unclear. Some believe it was introduced in the latter part of the eighteenth century, probably by Russians, and others claim it had existed well before that. Certain Native groups believed it was carried by caribou.

No one denied that the disease had spread, slowly but mercilessly. In the early 1930s, a medical survey found that more than a third of Native deaths were attributable to TB. Few Native families escaped death, crippling, or disability from the disease. By the mid-1940s, TB was believed to be even more entrenched in rural Alaska.

If he was going to motivate a letter-writing public, Albrecht knew he needed facts and a persuasive message. The Alaska Tuberculosis Association, a private, voluntary group, had arranged for x-rays to diagnose infected people in Anchorage, but had not compiled statistics. More useful were BIA surveys showing an annual TB death rate among Natives anywhere from six hundred to one thousand cases per hundred thousand people. If true, this meant Alaska was caught in an epidemic.

"These were valuable numbers for me, and I also saw that we had an opportunity to do something about the disease now that the war was over," Albrecht recalled. "There were army and navy hospitals in Alaska that were no longer needed and could be made available for isolation and care. As it was then, patients had to be sent Outside. Here was a great chance, if we could pull it off, to attack the spread of this disease right here at home."

With fervor in his voice and conviction in his message, Albrecht visited every podium available. Rotary clubs, Kiwanis, chambers of commerce, churches, every civic organization throughout the territory that would listen to him heard his speech about the frightening prevalence of tuberculosis. Each talk included a vigorous plea to write the governor, urging swift attention.

And the letters came, by the basketful. Albrecht had carried out his charge with not only aplomb but notable results. Now, in the governor's study, he and Gruening met to thrash out a bill to present to the legislature, asking for an appropriation and the powers that would launch the war on TB.

The governor was elated with the public response, but he knew the legislature could be obstreperous and that he had enemies there who would oppose any program he proposed.

"The letters are impressive but let's not take any chances," he advised Albrecht. "We need a strategy that will inspire the legislators to provide the dollars we need for your health program, something that will have strong public appeal." Then he threw out a few ideas: What if the agenda also included benefits for the veterans of World War II? Wouldn't that arouse public interest? Wouldn't legislators be more inclined to act?

Gruening was earnest in his ploy. The governor was as anxious to assist the veterans as he was to provide a sound health program for the territory. In March 1945, he had urged the legislature to create a development board for veterans, as every state in the union had done, and to enact other benefits.

At the same time, he had asked for a Department of Health with a full-time commissioner and funds to combat what he called "the shocking incidence of tuberculosis." The governor well recognized the appalling state of health conditions in the territory. When half the Native men applying for military service during World War II were found to be physically unfit, usually because of tuberculosis, the evidence was undeniable.

The 1945 veterans' bill passed the Alaska House but was routed to a Senate committee which buried it for the entire session, giving as its reason that the war was not yet over. The legislature did create a new Department of Health with a full-time commissioner, but the appropriation for the program was a meager $30,000. The governor, dissatisfied with the funding, vowed to be smarter next time.

His new strategy was to call a special session of the Seventeenth Territorial Legislature for March 1946 to revive the veterans' bill and seek more money for the health agency. He would have two trump cards: The veterans would have returned to civilian life, eager to add their substantial political pressure, and he would have on hand his new health commissioner. Gruening knew how effective Albrecht could be at a rostrum.

There was suspicion about the true motives for the special assembly. Robert B. Atwood, writing in the *Anchorage Daily Times*, agreed "the facts and figures presented by the territorial health authorities are an indictment concerning all of Alaska. The problem they present is serious.

"On the other hand," he continued, "there are those who are convinced that certain political powers are using the tuberculosis problem as an excuse for convening the legislature. It is contended that the real purpose is not to remedy the tuberculosis problem but to embarrass those members of the legislature who are not political bedfellows.

"It is contended, and there is some reason to expect, that the call for the proposed special session would contain more than just the health problem," Atwood wrote. "It would probably list legislation for returning veterans, road construction, and possibly an income tax . . ."

Atwood, who consistently supported Albrecht throughout his tenure, supported him now but acknowledged "the background of politics throws a shadow" over the proposal and the fifteen-day special session could also "run into some hot political cross-fire."

Albrecht needed all the forceful oratory and decisive arguments he could summon to override such fears as he laid his case before the legislature. Although his eloquence rose to the challenge, it was what Gruening called "his effective presentations of the facts" that won the day. The appalling figures of tuberculosis, its entrenched history and egregious treatment plus the opportunity to acquire surplus military hospitals aroused the senators and representatives.

On March 15, legislators unanimously gave the department $250,000, a whopping appropriation in 1946. The grant was one-tenth of the territory's total budget. In less than one year, the territory's first full-time commissioner of health had won an unprecedented victory. As Atwood predicted, the session also passed a bill providing for many veterans' benefits and new taxes to pay for them.

The legislature gave Albrecht's new department full authority over the campaign against tuberculosis through whatever means it deemed appropriate. It encouraged and promoted the acquisition of adequate sanatorium facilities within the territory, provided for the cost of care and transportation elsewhere until those facilities were available, and opened access to obtaining surplus property useful to the program.

Overjoyed, Albrecht failed to note an undercurrent of hostility in the chambers, however. The coup marked the beginning of political resentment that would dog him all his days in office. The salmon canning industry, the backbone of Alaska's economy, was vocal in its opposition to taxation for improved health care. Legislators who were not as successful in obtaining funding for their own causes resented the doctor with the altruistic motives and fluent rhetoric. His increasing power baffled and irritated them. Eventually the envy would ripen into attack.

However, Albrecht was filled with optimism and enthusiastic ideas. "Now we can go to Washington, D.C., and ask for matching money," he told his staff excitedly. With luck, he said, the department might get $400,000.

Incredibly, in its regular term the following year, 1947, the legislature surpassed the special session, awarding the Department of Health $440,000 for health and sanitation. To Albrecht's delight the appropriation was made in a lump sum. "This gave me much greater latitude in budgetary decisions," he said.

The commissioner knew the largesse of the Alaska legislature would have a crucial impact in Washington, D.C. The federal government would be obliged to view the appropriations as evidence the territory acknowledged it own responsibilities. This was the sort of hometown behavior congressmen admired, he realized. But, loyal Gruening disciple that he was, he was not about to trade on that alone. Federal officials would require more convincing.

His strategy was to get corroborating proof of the disgraceful status of Alaska health. Perhaps, he reasoned, his own voice had been heard too often in the halls of government. Perhaps it was time for others to plead his case. As he said later, "Our methodology was to get some authorities other than those of us on the scene to support our cause."

One authority he chose was the American Medical Association, and the move was among his more illustrious political maneuvers. First, he had to convince the AMA that health problems in faraway and insignificant Alaska merited the attention of that august body. Then, he had to persuade J. A. Krug, secretary of the interior, to request and finance an investigation. Once again, his zeal, reasoning, and rhetoric carried the day. In July 1947, a team of five doctors arrived in Alaska to study the health situation.

To make certain the team saw the whole miserable picture, Albrecht himself, along with his tuberculosis consultant, Dr. Leo (Lee) J. Gehrig, guided the AMA group on a three-week, six-thousand-mile tour from Ketchikan to Barrow, visiting Native villages and talking with Alaska Native Service doctors and nurses as well as private physicians and Native leaders.

The investigators were Dr. Arthur Bernstein, chairman of the team, and Drs. Harry E. Barnett, Jack Fields, George Milles, and Joseph Silverstein, all members of the staff of Cook County Hospital in Chicago. Gehrig recalls the team allowed time to fish. "Those fellows from Chicago had never seen anything like the Alaska salmon," he said. "It was one of the highlights of the trip for them."

The physicians found the spread of tuberculosis so severe that they described it as "the most urgent and important health problem in Alaska." Dr. Bernstein reported, "The tuberculosis problem in the Territory of Alaska is more than alarming. It is unbelievable."

The revelations shocked the team. "We have found figures in Alaska that are hard for medical men to believe," Dr. Bernstein said. In one day in Bethel alone the specialists came across six active cases, none of whom could be hospitalized for lack of beds. In Kotzebue, Dr. E. S. Rabeau told them he had cared for forty patients with tuberculosis meningitis in just seventeen months. Half of the eighty-five who had died of TB in the past two years had been under the age of sixteen, Rabeau said.

The team estimated there were at least forty-five hundred cases of open pulmonary tuberculosis in Alaska with an incidence rate of 25 percent of the population infected in some villages. In Barrow, a teacher reported that of thirty children who entered school between the ages of five and six, only six had lived to finish high school. The others had died of tuberculosis.

At the conclusion of the three-week trip, the AMA team recommended that one thousand beds be made available for TB patients immediately. The team also called for opening a hospital in Anchorage with four hundred beds reserved for TB patients.

"Alaska does not know how fortunate it is to have men like Dr. Albrecht, Dr. Gehrig, Dr. Rabeau and Dr. Howard C. Rufus of the Alaska Native Service," Dr. Bernstein noted. "These men are doing yeoman service but they can't do the tremendous job without help or funds. Our committee in its recommendation will give them every possible backing."

Albrecht himself could not have written a more favorable prescription. With his case now strengthened by the AMA recommendations, he decided to lay before Congress his plea for more funding for health and sanitation improvements.

Albrecht planned carefully for his foray to Washington, D.C., in 1948. First he spent many hours with the U.S. Public Health Service, detailing the extent of tuberculosis and other medical troubles in Alaska. Then, using a Gruening tactic, he sought out Rep. Frank Keefe of

Wisconsin, an important member of the House Appropriations Committee and described as "hard-bitten and tight-fisted." Albrecht paid Keefe the honor of consulting with him privately before meeting with other members of Congress.

Gruening and Alaska's new congressional representative, Edward Lewis "Bob" Bartlett, went with Albrecht and let him do the talking.

"His presentation had a crusading spirit to it," Bartlett said later. "Under the spell of Earl's arguments, the congressman's heart opened like a blossom in spring."

Keefe was won over. "It's time to approach these Alaska health problems in a realistic manner," he announced. He promised to call hearings immediately to hear the testimony. Keefe had no trouble moving the hearings to an early end and producing a favorable report.

In its conclusion it stated, "After giving careful consideration to the evidence and the suggested program, the committee has determined to provide a health program (in Alaska) on an emergency basis as a direct operation of the Public Health Service, to be operated in a manner similar to emergency health programs around military installations in this country during the last war."

The report continued, "Rather than appropriate an amount sufficient for the full fiscal year, the committee has provided $700,000 on an eight-month basis and will want to review the entire matter after the convening of the next Congress in light of developments by that time and the projected need for appropriations for the ensuing year as the situation at that time may warrant."

In June 1948, Congress approved an appropriation of $1,115,000 for health and sanitation needs in Alaska, far more than the $400,000 Albrecht had dared to anticipate. Once again, he came away with his pockets bulging with dollars, and this time it was from the U.S. Congress. His political acumen was growing.

Albrecht's familiarity with federal bureaucracy, plus his determination to consummate his health program, inspired him to gather support from all the sources he could tap. He coerced the BIA to lend a voice to his requests for funding. He won special grants from the U.S. Children's Bureau for maternal and child health and for the care of crippled children, a major national concern given the prevalent tuberculosis and poliomyelitis.

Governor Gruening gave him advice about the power system.

"He would say to me when I would go back to D.C. twice a year, 'Earl, the Democrats are in power now, but the Republicans are going to be in someday. I want you to visit the Republican minority, keep them abreast. That's just good politics, down-the-road planning.'

"And he was right," Albrecht said. "I got to know the Republican congressmen, some of whom couldn't have cared less about Alaska, but they kept hearing from me, and when their party came into power, they remembered me."

The commissioner's fund-raising success was, however, only a part—although a most important part—of his accomplishments in his first few years in office. While he campaigned for funds to erase tuberculosis, he had devised a four-pronged attack on TB as soon as he was named to head the health department and he began putting it to work even while his annual budget was small.

His plan was to first determine the full extent of TB, then to provide treatment, next to educate all of Alaska about the disease, and, finally, to rehabilitate all patients. These were his goals from the start; his faith in his mission was such he was certain the money would come.

If it took a little politics to make the dream a reality, he was up to that, too.

# CHAPTER 7
# Tracking Down TB

*The floating clinic aboard M/S* **Hygiene II** *brought tuberculosis screening to coastal Alaskans.*

On a cool September day in 1945, with summer slipping away and the aspen leaves turning gold, Commissioner Albrecht, new on the job, sighed as he looked over the mounting paperwork on his desk, lifted his hat from its rack, and headed out the door at the Department of Health.

"I'm going out to check on something," he announced to no one in particular. Most of the department desks were empty; the staff was so short-handed that employees were usually out in the field. They worked in the office only when paperwork could no longer be ignored.

Albrecht made his way to Twelfth Street leading to the waterfront. He noted with a grimace the refuse on Juneau's streets and wondered if some public health ordinance might be cited to clean it up. "These people don't appreciate what a beautiful place Alaska is," he grumbled to himself.

His mood soon improved. The air was fresh, the sky a clear blue, and before him the waters of Juneau Harbor sparkled in the sun. He was beginning to adapt to the capital city. In the absence of a Moravian church, he had found a Methodist church he liked, and he had settled into a comfortable home with his family. The Rev. Frederick P. McGinnis, his pastor, recalls the Albrecht residence, in the center of town, was "modest but elegant." Blanche delighted in entertaining there and even when her frequent migraine headaches kept her in bed, Earl took over as host. Jane and Jack were active in the church, as was Earl, and there were frequent parties at the governor's mansion just up the hill. Yes, Juneau had its appeal, Albrecht admitted, as he strode briskly, keeping his eye on the boats riding at anchor.

He was looking for the F/S *Hygene*, the health department's floating medical clinic that had proved, in its six-month history, to be a boon to Southeast Alaska. The ship, staffed with nurses and physicians, had visited Hoonah, Sitka, Wrangell, and Petersburg. Dr. C. C. Council, Albrecht's predecessor as one of the rotating part-time health department commissioners, had conceived of the *Hygene* and the unusual spelling of its name.

Albrecht loved the idea of the floating clinic. Since so many Alaskans lived along waterways, it made sense to bring health care by boats. He had never seen the *Hygene* but he had heard of it, heard of its enthusiastic acceptance, particularly by Native people. If it works for Southeast, why can't it work for all coastal Alaska, he asked himself. Already he could envision a route to the Aleutians, up the Bering Sea, maybe even up the Yukon and Kuskokwim rivers. He itched to get the project going.

On the pier, a lone figure stood tamping a pipe. Albrecht approached him and asked, "Can you tell me if the *Hygene's* one of those boats out there?"

The man looked Albrecht over carefully. "Bet you're a doctor," he said. "*Hygene's* a doctor boat. You goin' on the *Hygene?*"

"No," Albrecht answered. "I just want to know which one it is."

"That one," the fellow said, gesturing with his pipe. "The one with the stripes on the side."

Albrecht's heart sank. The boat was scarcely more than fifty feet long. "Why," he said, "it's really nothing more than a, than a . . . "

"Than a cutter, right?" the man said. "Used to be a yacht."

Still is a yacht, Albrecht thought dejectedly. No wonder it never sailed farther than Ketchikan. This was not the kind of craft that could withstand the brutal Bering Sea, ride out the gales of the Aleutians. It's fit only for the sheltered straits of Southeast Alaska, he conceded gloomily.

With a heavy step, Albrecht headed back to his office, his dream of waterborne medical care for thousands of Alaskans left behind on the pier. Still, he believed the concept was a sound one. All he needed was money.

When the territorial legislature created the full-time post of commissioner of health in the spring of 1945, its philanthropy was in short supply. Only $30,000 was appropriated, with the assumption the funds were sufficient to eliminate tuberculosis in the territory. Gruening and Albrecht knew the sum was hopelessly inadequate. In time and with shrewdness and exhaustive effort, Albrecht would acquire the necessary funding, but in his early days in office his budget was depressingly small.

The new commissioner also learned quickly that his staff was inadequate for its tasks. He was beginning to think Alaska would be forever shortchanged. Certainly his days in Palmer, where he had financed his own wearisome trips to the nation's capital to save his hospital, had convinced him that few in federal power took the distant land seriously. Only its strategic military location seemed to give it any credence. It looked as though it was time, once again, for him to wage his own campaign if he was to have any sort of success as a health commissioner.

Albrecht was willing to carry out Gruening's order to spread the message about tuberculosis—in fact, he spent much of his early months as commissioner lecturing on the threat of the disease—but he was not willing to wait for the legislature to reconvene and hope for a bigger budget. Nor did he place much faith in Gruening's plan to call a special session as a means of acquiring greater funding. The big money lay Outside, Albrecht had found—in the Congress and in the large charitable foundations.

In December 1945, he decided he could no longer run his office as he wished without an infusion of money or personnel. With the Congress and his own legislature on hold, he headed for the source he felt most likely to help, the National Tuberculosis Association in New York. With its single focus on the problem, surely it was the most logical source for help.

The TB association saw it differently. "We never fund grants for states," Albrecht was told, "but we know the situation in Alaska is extremely severe so we'd be willing to loan you a specialist. We could even pay some of the salary."

"How much of the salary?" Albrecht asked.

"One-quarter," was the answer.

"If you can make it one-third, I think I can get the Alaska Tuberculosis Association to pay one-third and the territorial legislature to pay one-third," Albrecht said evenly. He had learned something of the art of negotiating and now put it to work. The Alaska TB Association already had earmarked $11,625 for Albrecht to use in obtaining matching funds for tuberculosis control. And it would have contributed $5,410 for departmental x-rays of high school students, but the lack of equipment reduced the expenditure to less than $1,000. The agency also paid rehabilitation costs of Alaska tuberculosis patients in hospitals in the state of Washington, and had allocated $5,000 for patient care and $3,000 for crippled children's expenses.

The compromise was sealed with a handshake. Albrecht was referred to Lois Jund, who had been an intern with the national TB association and who had a graduate degree in public health administration from Yale University. She was on leave from the New York office and working as a health director at the army's Signal Security Headquarters in Arlington, Virginia.

When Albrecht called to arrange a meeting the following day, he had no idea that his timing was right on the money. Jund's duties had been reduced since the end of the war, and she worried about future employment. Albrecht's call caught her interest. After an interview the next day at the Bellevue Stratford Hotel in Philadelphia, Albrecht wrote Jund offering her the position of TB control director in his department. She wrote back her acceptance although she was uncertain about the wisdom of it all. She was just twenty-three.

Jund arrived in Juneau on Valentine's Day 1946, a cold, rainy night. "There was no one at the airport to meet me, nor had any plans been made for where I might stay," Jund recalled. "A cab driver took me to the Baranof Hotel, and the next day I went to the Alaska TB Association. Bess Winn, secretary of the TB association, said, 'I don't know why you're here, but any help is welcome.' That didn't sound right so I went to the health department and found no one there knew about me, either. Albrecht was off in the field and apparently had not told anyone I had been hired. I began to wonder what I had gotten myself into."

Her experience turned out to be typical personnel policy for C. Earl, as his staff called him. Bringing people into the department from within and without Alaska, he often forgot to inform his staff of the hire, and occasionally even promised the same job to more than one candidate.

John and Betsy Tower, both graduates of Yale Medical School, remember Albrecht on a staff-hunting mission. He arrived at their New Haven, Connecticut, home, sporting wide red suspenders and carrying his belongings in a box tied with rope.

"We were in our last year of residency at Grace New Haven Community Hospital, John in pediatrics," Betsy Tower recalled. "Albrecht needed a pediatrician to qualify for federal funding from the Crippled Children's Association. He held out lots of carrots, and since John had wanted to go to Alaska anyway, we accepted. But when John reported to the department in Juneau he found three other physicians had been hired for the same job!"

John Tower eventually served as a consultant to the U. S. Public Health Service but was chiefly occupied with his own Anchorage pediatrics practice, which was swamped by an epidemic of polio.

Albrecht's work also was hampered by a shortage of qualified personnel willing to work in the Bush. He was an accomplished fisherman and hunter—handsome trophies of bear and sheep graced the walls of his home—and he also became skilled hunting dedicated people to share his commitment to Alaska. Coaxing, coercing, and hawking

the natural glories of the territory, dangling tempting opportunities for professional growth, appealing to whatever
indications of altruism he could detect, he managed with
considerable personal effort to assemble proficient, hard-
working teams.

It was not an easy sell. Undeveloped postwar Alaska
was hardly a magnet for medical specialists nor was the
pay enticing. It drew those spirited souls willing to invest
a few years living in the Last Frontier, but there were never
enough of them, and many were young novices. The only
way Albrecht could attract experienced physicians was to
allow them the right to private practice while working for
the Department of Health.

He tried to show likely candidates that life in Alaska
could be close to Utopia. At least, it was for him. His free
time was increasingly squeezed by his administrative duties,
but he still managed to slip away on weekend camping
trips with Jack. He discovered that Lois Jund had acquired
a ten-foot skiff with an outboard motor, and he coerced
her to take him fishing, usually with Dorothy Whitney
along. Lois found him a creditable fisherman but poor with
the net. "He cost me the biggest salmon I ever hooked into
because he handled the net wrong," she recalled.

Meanwhile, the U.S. Public Health Service, recogniz-
ing Alaska's plight in attracting seasoned professionals,
assigned Dr. Leo (Lee) J. Gehrig to the department early in
1946. Later, through the service, Albrecht acquired Dr.
Robert L. Smith, also trained in treatment of TB.

Sometimes Albrecht got lucky within the territory, as
he did with Amos Joseph "Joe" Alter, a commissioned public health officer with the U.S. Public Health Service in
Juneau. Albrecht met Alter shortly after arriving in Juneau.
He was instantly taken with the gregarious health officer.
He soon learned that Alter had qualities more interesting
than charm.

One of Alter's duties, Albrecht discovered, was disposing of surplus military equipment, since the health service in wartime was an arm of the military. Albrecht told Alter he urgently needed a vessel for his projected marine clinic and asked him to keep the health department in mind if a ship became available.

Alter had yet another virtue: He was a graduate of Purdue University with a degree in sanitary engineering. Problems with water supplies and waste disposal in the Bush were almost as appalling as the state of tuberculosis. The commissioner sorely needed an expert to address the widespread problem. Such a find in remote Alaska seemed a gift from heaven. Albrecht could not afford to let him escape.

Alter, who had told his wife they would be going back to Indiana as soon as his public health stint was ended, succumbed to Albrecht's sales pitch and joined his staff as director of environmental health and sanitation. His first assignment was to survey Bush sanitation. His report identified gross defects in both the supply of clean water and the disposal of waste, particularly in villages where the ground remained frozen year-round.

"People just dipped out water wherever they could find it and often had to melt ice and snow," Alter recalls. "Human wastes and garbage were usually just thrown in the nearest river. Such practices contributed mightily, of course, to the spread of disease."

Albrecht, well aware of the insidious link between poor sanitation and tuberculosis, knew the value and significance of Alter's findings. Now he had two good reasons to be grateful to his sanitation expert. While still a captain in the U.S. Public Health Service, Alter had fulfilled Albrecht's dream of waterborne health care for Alaska's coastal towns. In his final days with the health service, Alter had handed over to the health department a 128-foot boat used during the war for freight and personnel transportation. It gave Albrecht his coveted floating clinic.

The vessel needed reconditioning to provide labs, x-ray rooms, examining rooms, dental offices, and quarters for the crew. This required money. Here, Albrecht found a use for the old F/S *Hygene*. Its sale paid for renovations aboard the larger boat. When Jund arrived in Juneau, he proudly showed her the M/S *Hygiene II* (this time spelled correctly) in Juneau Harbor.

When the legislature's special session in 1946 allocated $250,000 to fight tuberculosis, and added $440,000 the following year, Albrecht finally had the capital to launch his all-out campaign in every Alaskan community.

His frontal assault focused first on the coastal communities. The seagoing *Hygiene II* was "just right," he recalled. "It had a big fifty-foot-by-fifty-foot hold that we had rebuilt into a clinic. It was large enough for a doctor, a nurse, a lab technician, a dentist, and a dental assistant. Now we had a real unit that could visit places like Homer, Kodiak, Seward, the Aleutians, the Bering Sea coast, as well as all of Southeast. We could go for at least six months at a time. Eventually, we stayed out all year.

"Then we converted two barges—the M/V *Yukon Health* and the *Hazel B*—to do the same kind of work. Put great big outboard engines on them and sent them up the Yukon and Kuskokwim rivers," Albrecht says. The medical teams went up as many of the Kuskokwim's 540 miles and the Yukon's fourteen hundred miles (to the Canadian border) as possible before winter and ice set in. Youngsters, enduring the vaccinations that were dispensed, dubbed the vessels "shot ships."

The Kuskokwim route led through central western Alaska, to settlements at Bethel and other villages occupied chiefly by Yupik Eskimos. On the Yukon River, the *Yukon Health* reached into the Interior and Western Alaska sites of Athabaskan Indians and small colonies of Yupik and Inupiat Eskimos.

Albrecht's second battle plan used the Alaska Railroad from Seward to Fairbanks and its spur tracks. He purchased two railroad cars, outfitting one as a clinic and the other as housing for the staff.

"In those days the railroad was the only way on land to get from Fairbanks to Seward," Albrecht said, "and our clinics stopped at every town and hamlet along the way. They would be pulled up to Wasilla, go up to Curry on the side track, and everyone in town would be x-rayed."

The trains demanded extraordinary sacrifice from the staff in wintertime. Dr. Smith, on loan to Albrecht from the U.S. Public Health Service, was especially sympathetic with the dentists, who labored in cramped offices and with an imperfect heating system.

"Heat came in from the ceilings," Smith recalled, "and the poor dentist had to work with his head in 95-degree temperatures and his feet on ice-cold floors, and sometimes actually on ice."

Then there were the people living along the territory's limited road system to be surveyed. "We had a highway unit, a truck fixed up with an x-ray unit and a doctor, a lab technician, and a nurse, and that went into homes on the Glenn Highway and the Richardson Highway," Albrecht said. "These health workers had to stay at roadhouses or any other place they could find lodging. It was a mission of mercy.

"And then, to be certain we were reaching as many Alaskans as absolutely possible, we had a plane that carried large trunks of x-ray equipment and a technician to remote villages," he said.

The logistics of acquiring and outfitting the mobile clinics were not as fearsome as was acquiring and outfitting the medical teams. Albrecht called for help from Dorothy

Whitney, the long-time territorial nurse supervisor he had worked with in Anchorage and Palmer. Albrecht had made her director of the Division of Public Health Nursing soon after his appointment.

Whitney sent out offers to all competent nurses she knew, among them Catherine "Kitty" Smulling. Smulling, who later married Angus Gair, had worked for Whitney in Anchorage in 1942 and 1943 and was now back in her home town of Altoona, Pennsylvania. Trained at Jefferson Hospital in Philadelphia, she had been taking courses at the University of Pennsylvania but was homesick for Alaska. Whitney had little trouble coaxing her to return and join the battle.

"I got back to Alaska in 1946, and my first trip was out to the Aleutians," Kitty Gair said. "The second year, I went to the Bering Sea, to Nome and up to St. Lawrence Island, and then to Western Alaska. Then we toured Southeast Alaska. Once, when we went out to Dutch Harbor in the Aleutians, we came at just the right time because the navy was ready to dump some medicines in the bay, and instead they gave them to us."

The five years Gair spent on the *Hygiene II*, from 1946 to 1951, showed her a side of nursing that only Albrecht's floating clinics could produce.

"Our main purpose was to track down the TB cases, to treat them, and to provide education about health, and immunize the children," Gair recalled. "We would go ashore when we could, if there was a deep enough harbor, but the *Hygiene* had too much draft to go close to shore, so sometimes we had to anchor six or seven miles offshore. Then, either we had to go ashore in boats, or the people had to row out. And then they had to climb rope ladders to get on board. Later, they made a sort of landing platform that made it easier.

"Many times the seas were so rough and stormy that

we couldn't get to shore and no one could get out to us,"
she said. "And if any of us were on shore or any patients
aboard the ship, everyone had to stay where they were,
sometimes for several days, until the storm subsided. When
I was marooned and couldn't get back to the ship I stayed
with the teachers; they were wonderful.

"We would stay at the villages anywhere from three
days to six weeks, depending on the size of the population. We often worked until 2 a.m. to take advantage of the
summer light."

The team took x-rays of every willing villager—man,
woman, and child—and nearly all were willing. The tuberculosis toll was better known by the Natives than anyone
else, although even they had no idea of its proportions,
nor did they understand the nature of the disease.

"We awakened them to the danger of the spread of TB,
to the availability and importance of care and their own
responsibility as a community," Gair said.

In the program's early days and in Albrecht's urgency
to determine how serious the spread of TB was, the clinic's
teams were induced to work quickly so they could visit as
many communities as possible. The pace frustrated the
professionals, who wanted to treat all the physical problems they encountered, not only tuberculosis. There were
epidemics of diphtheria and polio to be addressed, decayed
teeth to be pulled, babies to be delivered. It defied all their
medical training to forsake such needs.

"We wanted to stay and give a generalized program,"
Gair said. "And leaving too soon meant we were gone before the x-rays were developed, so we could only send a
letter back to those infected. It was very inefficient in the
beginning." Even when x-rays were developed on the spot,
they were sent to laboratories in Anchorage, Fairbanks,
and Juneau for further interpretation, which took precious
time.

Albrecht recognized more time was needed to deal with patients' health needs. In subsequent trips, the teams stayed until all x-ray results were in. Then those with active sputum could be isolated, always a strange and disturbing procedure for the Natives, who lived communally.

"We had to teach isolation as much as possible, to hang sheets between beds, and this was hard on these people who often slept in one bed because there weren't enough blankets to go around," Gair said. "We told the people we would try to find places for them, but Alaska had so few available hospital beds at that time that most of the patients just had to stay at home in some sort of an isolation.

"This led to a lot of distrust on the part of the Natives. The second and third years around we had difficulty establishing rapport because we hadn't been able to get their sick members into a sanatorium. We had to build trust all over again. But any resentment always disappeared before we left.

"They had no understanding of the importance of cleanliness," she recalled. "They used dishcloths until they literally fell apart, never used soap for washing dishes, never rinsed them. We had to teach them to spit into a can and not on the floor, where they delivered their babies, or in the street, where children played. We had to warn them to take their water from upstream rather than downstream."

The doctors gave examinations to entire families, and Gair conducted health classes, prenatal classes, and well-baby clinics, but here language was a problem. "We had to have health materials in five languages—Aleut, Eskimo, Filipino, Indian, and English," Gair said. "The Natives' cultural habits, superstitions, and their economy also posed difficulties. For example, people would say, 'How much are you paying us to go out to your boat?' We told them we weren't there to pay them, we were there to help them, but wouldn't charge them. After a while they appreciated that, but it was something of a bone of contention before it was settled."

It was heartening for Gair and others in the mobile units to note, as the program progressed, the Natives' growth in knowledge and responsibility. "It was reassuring to see the attitude of the people change," she said. "Where once they just sat and smiled while we instructed them in good health care, in later visits they spoke freely and asked questions and indicated they really understood what was being taught."

Before Albrecht's armadas appeared on the scene, Lois Jund prepared the communities for what was to come. She had the formidable task of being the commissioner's advance agent, selling his plan to track the TB invasion throughout Alaska. For the first year and a half of the mobile system, she traveled everywhere from Ketchikan to Barrow, getting each community ready for whatever type of health unit would follow—a ship, train, truck, plane.

"I would go into each village and start with the teachers, who were absolutely essential and accommodating in helping us," Jund said. "They would have a roster of every inhabitant and usually some information about them. They helped us round up teenage volunteers who would work for the incoming teams, they would secure a place for the examinations and x-rays and they were the ones who gave me a place to sleep. The only trouble with this was they were so hungry for company from Outside they would keep me up all night, talking!"

At one point in her assignment, Jund was gone from Juneau for nine months, traveling from village to village, often by dubious means and in perilous weather. "Once I was in Naknek waiting for a plane to take me to King Salmon," Jund said, "and after waiting for hours and hours I finally got another pilot to fly me there. After I landed, I learned the reason the first plane didn't pick me up was because it had crashed in a river and both the pilot and passenger had been killed. Mine was not an easy job."

None of the jobs with the mobile system was easy. The illnesses the medical teams encountered were profuse, varied, complex, and often serious, taxing skills and ingenuity. The necessary medications and equipment often were unavailable. Compassion, patience, insight, and stamina were stretched thin. The vast expanses the teams covered meant long hours and risky travel. Weather, isolation, and rigorous living conditions added to the constant stress.

Yet, not all of it could have been tiresome pressure because two years after joining the *Hygiene II* crew, Kitty Smulling and the ship's chief engineer, Angus Gair, were married at the Methodist church in Juneau. A brief honeymoon followed in Washington, D.C., "because Angus had never been East," and then they returned to duty on the *Hygiene*.

"You might not think it possible, but being on the ship was actually a pretty romantic situation," Kitty Gair said with a grin.

CHAPTER 8

# Victory in Sight

*This mobile TB unit was among several reaching
families along the territory's road system.*

As the mobile units paced their way throughout Alaska, the new figures on tuberculosis arrived on Albrecht's desk. Among the first statistics from the M/S *Hygiene II*: 743 active cases found, including 308 Native males, 343 Native females, 69 white males, 23 white females. The numbers throughout the territory rose until 1954, the worst year for new cases, then began to drop as Albrecht gained control over the epidemic.

The total number of cases determined by the units eventually came close to the estimate of the AMA team: more than 4,000 for the territorial population of approximately

128,000. About 94,000 people lived in the Bush, where tuberculosis was running wild. The death rate was a grim 653 cases per 100,000 people. It was eight times the average of the Lower 48 and the highest in the world. More than 89 percent of the infected were Natives, although the rate for tuberculosis among the white population also was high—twice that of the rest of the nation.

Albrecht was not surprised. From observations during his army days when he visited outposts throughout the territory, from findings by the BIA, from reports of village clinics, he was braced for the bad news. In 1946, 43 percent of all death certificates for Indians, Eskimos, and Aleuts in Alaska listed tuberculosis as the cause. Albrecht suspected the epidemic might actually be worse than reported since death certificates often were signed by nonmedical people. He feared each misdiagnosed case may have spread to eight or nine new victims.

The death rate was highest among Eskimo males and lowest among white females. The disease hit hardest those in the ages from twenty-five to forty-four, then those from fifteen to twenty-four, lastly those from forty-five to sixty-four. The alarming statistics showed tuberculosis was taking a severe toll of Native parents and their teenage children, frequently debilitating entire families.

The mobile units gave the commissioner the necessary evidence to lay before territorial and federal appropriation committees, but his offensive had only just started. He could not wait for governmental bodies to act. He had to remove these active cases from the communities now. But where was he to put them?

In 1945, there was only one sanatorium in the territory, a 152-bed former army hospital in Skagway. It had been turned over by the military in April to Alaska Native Service, which opened it to non-Natives as well. The Sisters of St. Anne were contracted for nursing, and Dr. Rudolph M. Haas put in charge of medical duties by the U.S. Public

Health Service. He was the sole physician to supervise care of the entire patient load.

When Dr. Haas went on leave for several months in 1946, Albrecht replaced him with Dr. Gehrig. Albrecht was a virtuoso in ferreting out free assistance, whether it came in the form of money or people, and his appeal to the U.S. Public Health Service for personnel appealed to Gehrig's desire to see Alaska. He arrived with his wife just in time to take over briefly at Skagway.

Albrecht reorganized his department soon after taking office and established, among other sections, a Division of Tuberculosis Control. When Gehrig returned to Juneau from Skagway, he assumed direction of the division and gave much of his attention to the operation of the mobile units. One of his achievements in his two years in Juneau was a listing by name of every tubercular case. "It was like one enormous Rolodex," he said.

Gehrig had a specialty that was particularly valuable to the success of the program—he could read x-rays with a fluoroscope, a talent usually beyond the skills of the physicians aboard the marine clinics. He traveled with the boats for weeks at a time, training the crews and adding to the effectiveness and speed of the hunt for TB.

"People used to say to us, 'Why do you feel you have to scour the whole territory to find TB? Isn't there plenty of it right in plain view?' To which the answer had to be 'Yes,'" Gehrig said. "But that would not have been sufficient for Earl. He was a mover. He was not one to wait for things to come his way, to be approved before they were put into use. He went out and got what he wanted. Some people didn't like this; his aggressiveness really irritated them. But that didn't bother him. In the matter of TB, he wanted a full accounting and he insisted on getting it. Furthermore, he was determined to also get the hospitals these sick folk needed."

When Albrecht testified before the Alaska Legislature

at the special session in March 1946, he stressed the deplorable fact that only 289 beds were available for the many tuberculosis cases he was finding. And of these, 137 were in government and private hospitals and not necessarily reserved for TB patients.

Alaska welcomed the Skagway hospital, but it was hardly adequate to meet the demands. "The Skagway sanatorium is a first step in the right direction," Albrecht said in response to the donation. "So great is our problem, however, that the territory alone cannot assume the financial burden necessary for the eradication of tuberculosis. We need more help from the federal government. We need more doctors, nurses, and hospital attendants. Finally, we need more sanatoriums, enough to care for all the unattended cases, and toward that end we are working."

Albrecht keenly felt the anguish of Natives with advanced cases of TB. They were not only stricken with a possibly fatal disease but hospitalization Outside subjected them to strange ways, even a strange language in some instances, and separated them from their ancient customs, their families, all that was familiar to them.

"In the early days, it was painful to send people to a sanatorium, no matter where it was, because we were sending them there to die," he said. "We had no way to cure them, no drugs in those days. They realized this and it was a tremendous decision on their part. They were leaving Akutan, they were leaving the Tanana country, they were leaving the Yukon, the only places they had ever known.

"I always give credit to the Natives of Alaska," Albrecht emphasized, "because they saw what this disease, which they didn't understand, was doing to their families, to their population so that they were willing to let father or mother or brother or sister go off to a sanatorium, knowing they would never return. Why, we even sent some to Chicago—

where no one knew their Native language or served their Native foods—because that's where we could get some beds.

"Think what it was like," Albrecht said, "going into a village and finding that this one and that one had active, positive sputum. It was impossible to cure them, but they knew that by leaving it would keep the disease from spreading to the rest of the family. Those people deserve great credit for cooperating with the program, for being x-rayed and going to a sanatorium. The Natives were the real heroes of it all."

Dr. Frank Pauls, a bacteriologist who headed the laboratory at Anchorage, agreed. "We had authority only to quarantine, not to force people to go to a sanatorium," Pauls said. "That was a decision they had to make themselves. But they did have the hope that perhaps the sanatorium could make them well. And for that reason, and to spare their families, they almost always went."

Pauls, who later became chief of the state laboratories, says he marveled at the accord of Alaskans in the fight against tuberculosis.

"Their cooperation was superb," he said. "The public health nurses handed out sputum bottles like toothpicks and showed the people how to spit into them.

"Then the nurses sent them to us through the mail. We'd get sacks and sacks and sacks of these little bottles. Sometimes the sputum wouldn't go into the bottle but onto the outside so we at the lab had to be very careful how we handled it," Pauls said. "The best we could do with the staff we had was test about two hundred a day. Then we would send the information to Juneau for the record and back to the nurses, and in the positive or suspected cases there would follow a long process of further lab work."

Albrecht finally gained 159 more beds when the War Assets Administration turned over Fort Raymond Hospital in Seward to the territory in 1945. He had hoped to acquire the Fort Richardson hospital as well, had written voluminously to territorial senators and representatives to be poised to accept it but it never became available.

After frozen water lines were replaced at the Fort Raymond Hospital and the building converted to a sanatorium, it was leased to the Women's Division, Board of Missions, of the Methodist Church. Surplus x-ray equipment was donated by the U.S. Army, and the Women's Division financed the renovations. Dr. Annibal Roberto Valle was named superintendent by the U.S. Department of Public Health, and the first twenty-six patients were admitted July 7, 1946.

Albrecht needed hospital beds for a reason other than isolation. Tuberculosis often left its victims crippled and in constant pain. Every village had its share of people with deformities, and Albrecht was anxious to treat them, especially afflicted children.

He needed not only a special orthopedic facility but also surgeons and physical therapists trained in bone problems. And he wanted the hospital to be in Alaska so as to minimize disruption as much as possible for the young patients.

The answer came with another bonus of the military's wartime presence in Alaska. A surplus naval hospital with one hundred beds in the Mount Edgecumbe area of Sitka was being closed; Albrecht sought to have it transferred to his Department of Health. Congress, however, awarded the facility to the U.S. Department of the Interior, which was still in charge of the territory. Happily, Congress also appropriated funds for its operation and for an additional one hundred beds.

In 1946, the Interior Department turned over the hospital to Alaska Native Service, giving it full administrative jurisdiction, and signed a contract with

Albrecht's Department of Health for the hospitalization and care of patients.

Albrecht, deeply troubled as ailing Eskimos and Indians were wrenched reluctantly from their ancestral homes for the institutional care, frequently visited the hospitals to offer his encouragement and solace to the new patients. "You'll be here only a little while," he assured them as they fearfully took in their strange surroundings. "Soon you'll be back in the village with your families. Just let the doctors and nurses help you get well." It was more a hope than a certainty, more compassion than conviction.

With the acquisition of two hundred additional beds, Albrecht went on a hunt for trained personnel. As an enticement, he offered a six-month residency program under a physician on his staff and crossed his fingers in the hope that at least some of the interns would stay on board. A few did, serving in the territory's health centers.

Albrecht counted among his recruiting successes the hiring of Dr. Francis J. Phillips, whom he assigned to the Seward Sanatorium, and Dr. Philip H. Moore, an orthopedic surgeon who headed the crippled children's division at the Mount Edgecumbe Hospital.

Phillips had been a commanding officer of an army tent hospital in 1942-43 in the Aleutian campaign and was the first thoracic surgeon to practice in the territory. In his seven-year tenure in Seward he performed more than fifty major chest surgical operations each year plus hundreds of minor surgical procedures.

Phillips turned what had been planned as a tuberculosis sanatorium into a full-service hospital, dealing with a wide variety of medical problems at a cost of $10.46 per day per patient. Until the arrival of modern medicines, the hospital's TB treatment consisted of bed rest and usually surgically removing a rib and collapsing the lung. The greater majority of the approximately twelve hundred

Alaska tuberculosis patients at the Seward Sanatorium recovered and were sent home.

"Dr. Phillips introduced a wonderful program in rehabilitation," Albrecht recalled. "While he had these patients, sometimes for two years, he started to train them into certain aspects of life that were important. These dear folks didn't know anything about money, they didn't use it, so he put in a store. He let the patients work in the store, make change, sell things, buy things and develop their skills and crafts.

"It was also a part of their education," Albrecht said. "They didn't know TB was a communicable disease so he told them the simplest things to do and not do and he had charts and books in their characters—not the white man's characters—in a book that trained the Eskimo in healthy ways."

Phillips was a feisty little man whose independent style sometimes rankled hospital staff, but he had an affection for and understanding of his patients that helped make them well. Aware of the Natives' loneliness and homesickness, he inveigled the women of Seward to provide them with radios and magazines, cheerful visits, even birthday cakes.

"Without Dr. Phillips' consideration for the Natives, many would have bolted," Albrecht said. "Because he made their hospital stays as pleasant as possible, they remained for adequate treatment."

The Natives also remained because Albrecht made it possible for them to do so. Testifying on September 8, 1947, before the U.S. House Subcommittee on Territorial and Insular Affairs in Juneau, he noted that there were forty-eight Native patients at the Seward Sanatorium who might have to be moved because of a lack of funds.

"The Alaska Native Service was denied by the Senate of the United States Congress, in the last thirty-six hours of its session, the funds to pay for those patients," Albrecht told the subcommittee, "and the superintendent of Alaska Native Service must move those patients some six hundred miles to Juneau and to Sitka unless he has funds to pay for those patients."

Albrecht pointed out that Alaska's only thoracic surgeon was based in Seward and could not continuously travel to other hospitals to perform operations that would be lifesaving. "We do hope that you men will consider these things seriously and support us when you return to Washington," he concluded. His efforts were rewarded when ANS received sufficient funding for the patients the following month.

Albrecht was fiercely proud of the Sitka hospital's success with crippled children and he was determined to see it prosper. Opened in 1947, the facility was the first in Alaska to care specifically for the deformed; at that time it housed more cases of bone tuberculosis than any other facility in North America.

Albrecht had a high regard for Dr. Moore, whom he had brought from Oregon. Dr. Moore had done pioneering work there in treating the effects of crippling from tuberculosis.

"Moore is the one who developed the technique of taking the ribs that were thrown away by the thoracic surgeon and grinding them up and making a bone bank. It was a very unusual procedure," Albrecht said.

"The rib removed when the lung is collapsed is not infected with the bacillus and it is the perfect medium for doing bone grafting," Albrecht said. "Moore would freeze the ground-up bone and then go off to Kotzebue or Bethel where there were hospitals and operate on tuberculosis of the spine or the leg or the knee or the hip and use the bone as a graft.

"There were many hump-backed Eskimos at that time

and this was a graft that would help the bone heal. He used it for corrective surgery and it was a new thing in medicine, since usually bone grafts are taken out of the same patient. I'm certain he couldn't have been doing that kind of work in Chicago or Philadelphia," Albrecht said with a touch of pride.

Hospital stays could last years for difficult cases; Albrecht quickly recognized the need for education in the wards. He arranged with the BIA school at Mount Edgecumbe for classes that would prepare the patients for employment when they were released. They studied in their rooms—if necessary, in their beds—and learned how to type, solve math problems, and improve their reading. For diversion there was instruction in arts and crafts, with emphasis on Native traditions.

The Sitka and Seward sanatoriums gave Albrecht precious bed space, but the Skagway hospital, struggling under a shortage of nurses, was about to close. Its life span would be less than a year. Now he had to find some way to replace the beds that would be lost. "It took some real work with the Congress to get hospitals or support for the Native hospitals in Bethel, Barrow, Kotzebue, and other localities," Albrecht said. "We were always looking for help."

The AMA recommendation for a seven-hundred-bed hospital in Anchorage loaded Albrecht's gun with new ammunition. He did not hesitate to follow up on the report and to bring some important supporters into the ranks. He lined up Dr. Ralph B. Snavely, director of health for the BIA, and Dr. Edwin Norris, director of health for ANS, and added his powerful newspaper friend, Robert B. Atwood, publisher of the *Anchorage Daily Times*, to join him in taking his case for more health facilities to Congress once again.

Traveling to Washington had become somewhat easier

than in his Palmer days when he rode the plodding Alaska Railroad to Seward, then took the boat to Seattle and finally crossed the country by rail. But it still was an arduous trip. Beginning in the early 1940s, Pan American Airlines flew several times a week from Fairbanks to Juneau and then to Seattle where connections to points in the continental United States could be made. Although the turboprops took nearly ten hours to fly from Alaska to Seattle, Alaskans considered them a luxury. After a while, Albrecht stopped counting the interminable number of miles he traveled in service to Alaska.

Congress was not about to indulge the territory in the AMA prescription for a seven hundred-bed hospital, but in 1948, the Bureau of the Budget authorized Alaska Native Service to undertake preliminary planning for a four hundred-bed hospital somewhere in the Anchorage-Matanuska Valley area. Albrecht, disappointed in the reduced size, shrugged it off and concentrated on prodding the Department of the Interior to come up with funding for the project.

In 1949, Interior allocated $5,925,000 for construction, and when a fifteen-acre tract on Third Avenue in Anchorage was chosen over a rival site in Palmer, Atwood's *Anchorage Daily Times* announced the news in banner headlines.

Faulty construction delayed the official opening for more than half a year, but on November 29, 1953, the Alaska Native Medical Center was dedicated. It was the largest civilian building in Alaska and the final cost was more than $7 million, but the statistic that meant most to Albrecht was that the ANS bed capacity for the territory had nearly doubled.

The day after the dedication ceremonies, the hospital received its first patients, a man from Fairbanks and a woman from Teller, both with tuberculosis. Within a month

the hospital had 153 Bush patients, all with one form or
another of tuberculosis. In January 1954, less than two
months after the hospital opened, the institution was able
to hire enough staff to make 156 more TB beds available.
They, too, were immediately filled.

With the opening of the hospital, Albrecht began to
feel the tide turning against the epidemic. He had a good
supply of beds but, better yet, antibiotics had begun to
arrive. Dr. Robert Fortuine, a U.S. Public Health Service
physician who headed the Alaska Native Medical Center
from 1971 to 1977, says Alaska was fortunate in acquiring
the drugs early, almost as soon as they became available.

"Streptomycin was given in Alaska in 1948, although
since it was in very short supply, not all doctors had access to it," Fortuine said. "Then came the drugs PAS and
INH in the early '50s, and these were very effective. By
1952, physicians in Alaska were using all three, so Alaska
had a good head start on truly effective drug treatment for
tuberculosis."

Albrecht also advocated BCG, a vaccine that is a weak-
ened strain of the TB organism and given as a preventa-
tive. Developed in 1906 and first used in the 1920s, it was
popular in most European countries but not fully accepted
in the United States. A research program conducted in
Southeast Alaska by the U.S. Public Health Service showed
its success and inspired Albrecht to use it without qualms.

He also ordered that children be given routine tubercu-
lin tests that showed if they had been exposed or were
infected by the disease, although that did not necessarily
mean it was active. The Tine test, a simplified form of tu-
berculin testing, was also used for screening. Positive or
suspect reactions called for further diagnoses and, often,
drugs. With these salutary assists, tuberculosis was in retreat. Best of all, cured hospital patients were going home
to their villages.

"It took us several years before we could discharge people, get them well enough to go home, but it was a wonderful day when it happened," Albrecht said. "Within ten years, given a full accounting of all infected persons, modern hospital care, the establishment of health centers, and the use of new medicines, tuberculosis was in retreat.

"In the middle 1950s, it could happily be stated that tuberculosis in Alaska was under control. This did not mean there still were not many cases but it meant that when new cases were found and they needed hospitalization, there was no delay in getting them under active treatment. TB was not the dreaded scourge it had been, and an Eskimo baby had an increasingly better chance of surviving."

Albrecht had good reason for his cautious optimism that Alaskans were becoming healthier. Plenty of obstacles remained to be conquered, but he had learned how to achieve his aims and he had built a cadre of competent professionals. In the years since his arrival in Juneau, he had become a polished, formidable leader in the fields of both public health and politics.

However, he was about to lose the master who had trained him so well. The 1952 election had restored power to the Republican Party and put Dwight D. Eisenhower in the White House. Since the president appointed governors of U.S. territorial possessions, Gruening, an avowed Democrat, was out of office, and Republican B. Frank Heintzleman of Ketchikan, Alaska's regional forester in Juneau, was in. Life in the territorial capital henceforth would not be as felicitous for Albrecht.

In one of his last letters as governor, Gruening wrote in April 1953 to Reginald Atwater, executive secretary of the American Public Health Association, expressing his views on the federal government's attitude toward Alaska and on the accomplishments of his commissioner of health:

"The long standing neglect of the federal authorities in

respect to Alaska—who actually left us with no government at all for seventeen years and virtually no government for the first forty-five—was nowhere more flagrant
than in the field of health. There were no hospitals, no
clinics, almost no doctors, no therapy. Epidemics ravaged
the land. Every unhealthful condition known to modern
civilization existed in exacerbated form in Alaska.

"Before 1945, the only health organization in Alaska
was headed by a practicing physician who under the law
was permitted only to devote a part of his time to public
health—this in an area one-fifth as large as the United
States, and with the great variety of special climate and
ethnological factors which intensified the problem.

"As I am about to conclude thirteen years of eventful
service in the Governorship of Alaska, I feel it desirable to
write you that perhaps the greatest accomplishment during those years has been in the field of health. The progress
there is almost wholly due to one man, the present Commissioner of Health, Dr. C. Earl Albrecht."

Gruening went on to describe Albrecht's earlier medical career and his accomplishment of "near-miracles" in
the previous eight years. "The forces of disease and ill
health are in retreat," Gruening wrote, "but it is essential
that we do not relax and that we continue to press forward
under Dr. Albrecht's leadership with undiminished vigor
and enthusiasm."

Alaska, the governor wrote, is "not only a great outpost militarily and socially, but its destiny is to be in these
far northern latitudes a shining example of the American
way of life. It cannot be that as long as the incidence of
disease continues far higher than it should be in any civi-
lized country. We must make sure that that victory, now in
sight, is not only won but thereafter maintained."

As his friend stepped down from office, Albrecht realized Gruening had given a mandate not only to Atwater
but also to him.

# CHAPTER 9
# Health Care for All

*The Parran Team (Albrecht, center) found that health care in Alaska needed immediate improvement.*

As Albrecht contemplated his role during Ernest Gruening's administration, the previous eight years seemed to be a century. Had it been only eight years, he mused. He had come to his commissioner's appointment as a frontier physician, performing the mostly routine but sometimes heroic, duties of a family doctor. Now he was responsible for the general health of the entire territory. It was a formidable assignment, especially since Alaska had a history of deplorable medical care.

He could tick off a host of maladies that had riddled the territory for decades—hepatitis, influenza, pneumonia, venereal disease, meningitis, corneal opacities, typhoid fever, congenital heart disease, severely infected tonsils and adenoids, congenital malformations, cancer, mental illness, alcoholism, and more dental problems than the health department could possibly address.

Chronic otitis media, an inflammation of the middle ear, often with the lamentable aftermath of mastoiditis and even brain damage, was extremely common and a major concern. The Natives seemed especially vulnerable to accidents and fractures. Hundreds of surgical cases, often of long standing, desperately needed attention. And this was in addition to tuberculosis and its crippling effects.

Albrecht had an agenda as large as the territory. In addition to providing regular health services, he was responsible for sanitation and engineering, a full-time assignment in itself, as well as maternal and child health, nutrition, vision conservation, health education, public health laboratories, and recording Alaska's vital statistics.

It was a staggering array of challenges for the young department. It was also a heavy mandate for one overworked commissioner. Albrecht was always alert for any competent assistance he could find.

Attending a conference on tuberculosis in Detroit in 1949, his vigilance paid off. There, he met Dr. Robert L. Smith, trained in TB care and an officer in the U.S. Public Health Service, who was just finishing an assignment in New Orleans.

"How would you like to come to Alaska?" Albrecht inquired after telling impressive tales of the territory.

"I'd like it," Smith responded, "but I'm not sure the health service wants to send me there."

"Don't worry about that. I'll arrange things," Albrecht assured him, which he did without difficulty. This gave him the assistant he desperately needed, and Smith became his man in Anchorage, where the postwar population was rising steadily.

"We established weekly TB clinics and read the many x-rays that came from the marine units," Smith said. "We even tried to set up an Anchorage health department, giving free preschool physicals to children, but this did not set too well with the local doctors, and it was years before a health department was created there."

Still, Smith was able to provide an important base in Anchorage for health care in the Interior and to organize a nursing headquarters in Fairbanks. Smith's three years in the department, sharing responsibilities, also gave Albrecht welcome respite from the constant, arduous travel throughout the territory.

"I found it exciting to get around Alaska and even learned how to push seaplanes off sandbars," Smith said.

Alaska was playing catch-up after the war and after decades of neglect. Outsiders had brought diseases the Natives previously had been spared, but had not brought the means to treat them. The consequences during the nineteenth century were epidemics of smallpox, measles, and influenza plus outbreaks of typhoid, poliomyelitis, diphtheria, and other diseases. Those who escaped death from these diseases often faced weakness—making them unable to care for themselves or others—or even starvation.

Not until the early 1900s did the U.S. government acknowledge the need for health care in Alaska, and then it did so only minimally. The federal Bureau of Education sent a few doctors and nurses to the territory and opened small clinics in several Native villages. Medical services, for the most part, were dispensed by courageous, persevering itinerant nurses who covered the vast land by any possible means and dealt with impossible situations.

In 1910, the Bureau of Education opened a small

hospital, lasting only two years, in Juneau. In 1916 a more permanent facility for Natives opened in Juneau, and four more hospitals, three in the Interior and one in the Aleutians, were founded between 1917 and 1925. By 1930, the bureau had sixteen clinics and seven hospitals in the territory plus a floating clinic, the *Martha Angeline*, on the Yukon River.

In 1931, health care for Natives was transferred to the Bureau of Indian Affairs within the Department of the Interior. Conditions improved for the overworked itinerant nurses in that Natives now provided transportation between villages in exchange for nursing services, and the village teachers provided room and board. It was a sizable advancement over the days spent traveling by dog sled and sleeping at night in a cold tent.

This was the nursing picture Albrecht inherited when he assumed office in 1945, and it was not one that cheered him. He quickly contracted for more nursing help, began a program of special training in various fields of public health work, and named Dorothy K. Whitney chief of the public health nursing division.

By 1950, Albrecht had established full-time nursing services in every village of six hundred or more residents, and health centers in thirty communities. He had district laboratories in Anchorage, Juneau, Fairbanks, and Ketchikan, providing for rapid diagnosis of infections and diseases. But he worried about the hard-to-reach villages and especially about the infants born there.

Since Native women frequently gave birth at home, Albrecht turned his attention to midwifery and appointed Bertha B. Johnson to study and to attempt to meet the needs of these mothers.

Infant mortality for Alaska Natives produced tragic statistics—nearly eighty-seven babies out of one thousand born between 1952 and 1954 died in their first year and often at birth, an extremely high rate. Albrecht's charge to Johnson was to do what she could to change the gloomy picture, taking into account the various languages she would have to accommodate.

Her unique contribution was a series of booklets, profusely illustrated and with a minimum of English text, for use in the villages. They had such titles as *When Baby Is Born at Home* and *Your New Baby.* Johnson's *Manual for Alaska's Midwives* has become an international classic, has been translated into other languages and is distributed worldwide.

The outreach was so popular that Albrecht enlarged it in 1951 to establish home-birth classes in Northern, and later Southeast Alaska. As air service developed in the territory and more women flew to towns with hospitals for their deliveries, the program was revised to stress prenatal, postnatal, and infant care.

Forever seeking more help from the federal government, Albrecht had discovered other ways to get results. He had found it worked to rouse help from fellow advocates who wrote letters, made phone calls, and pressured power bastions. Throughout his career, he incited others to join his cause of the moment and use their influence on politicians. There was strength in numbers, he reasoned.

Best of all was the backing of experts, whose findings impressed the authorities and generated funds. The five AMA Chicago doctors, for example, had bolstered Albrecht's crusade significantly and enlightened Congress on the deplorable conditions in the territory. Buoyed by such support, Albrecht persuaded the Department of the Interior to send several teams to investigate conditions in Alaska.

The most effective of these by far was the Parran Team.

Under a contract with Interior, a quartet of public health authorities arrived in the territory in the summer of 1953. They were headed by Dr. Thomas Parran, dean of the University of Pittsburgh Graduate School of Public Health and the highly respected surgeon general of the Roosevelt era. The team returned for more detailed study in the summer of 1954 and published its report later that year.

Parran brought to the study not only his personal outstanding reputation but three distinguished University of Pittsburgh colleagues: Professors Antonio Ciocco, James A. Crabtree and Walter J. McNerney. During their initial visit they traveled more than six thousand miles and interviewed more than three hundred people.

In 1954, Parran and Crabtree returned, bringing with them Dr. Samuel M. Wishik, professor of maternal and child health. In this second visit, the scientists concentrated on problems the previous team had uncovered.

The final 279-page report was a scorching denunciation of the federal government as overseer of Alaska's health. The magnitude of tuberculosis alone was a scandal, the report stated, as was venereal disease, second only to TB as a health problem. Indeed, there was hardly a medical area that did not need immediate attention and improvement. The indifference of decades was producing shameful and monumental problems for the territory's people, it claimed.

The report made four major recommendations (and hundreds of other suggestions), leading with a call for an Alaska Native Service hospital under construction in Anchorage to open "without delay." Next it urged immediate steps be taken to improve Native village sanitation. A third recommendation was for help from the U.S. Public Health Service in augmenting "the grossly insufficient personnel for health care to the Natives." And lastly, it urged "active support of the Department of the Interior . . . in securing passage of legislation for much-needed revision of the present archaic and sometimes inhuman laws dealing with the commitment of the insane in Alaska."

Although the report did not mention Albrecht by name, it praised his accomplishments. Writing about "the incumbent, full-time Commissioner," it stated, "With characteristic energy, zeal and devotion of the crusader, he has applied himself to the task of building and organizing services and facilities necessary to meet some of the most urgent health needs of the Territory."

Then it made the laudatory statement that "No state health department in the United States has made such relative progress within a comparable period."

The intensity and scope of the report and the prestige of the scientists had the effect in Washington of a loud, ringing alarm. Congress quickly authorized $1,180,000 for Albrecht's department but, probably more importantly, the Department of the Interior was stung into greater respect for the territory's needs so that forthcoming requests were given quicker and fuller consideration.

Albrecht was uplifted, of course, by the findings but especially by its charge to the Department of the Interior to rectify treatment of Alaska's mentally ill. The situation was an infamy that had troubled him for years, going back to a disturbing memory from his Palmer days.

He had never forgotten the night in the autumn of 1935 when a group of men, remnants of the California contingent that had built homes for the colonists, knocked on his hospital door. The builders' own physician and most of the construction workers had departed the previous week, and Albrecht had agreed to provide any medical care that might be needed by the remaining crew.

"Doc, we've got a guy goin' nuts up at the camp," said

one of the delegation. "He's been like this ever since the others pulled out, sayin' he don't know what's going to happen to him, where he'll go now, things like that. He started tearing up the place yesterday, ripping apart his bed. Then he just sort of collapsed, sat in a corner all curled up, sucking his thumb even. Now he's fighting mad again. We can't do anything with him."

"Has he been drinking?" Albrecht asked.

"Naw, he don't touch a drop," said another of the group. "He's always been weird. Gets mad with everyone, eats alone, stares at ya like he hates ya. I just hope he doesn't get his hands on a gun. I think he'd let any of us have it. Can you give him a shot or something to calm him down?"

Albrecht knew whatever he could do to ease the situation would be temporary, but the construction camp was due to be closed in a few days. If he could tide things over, perhaps the man could find psychiatric help in the Lower 48. He collected his bag, checked it for the necessary supplies and headed for the camp, about a mile away.

However, the commotion had been heard by the colony. Albrecht and his escorts arrived to find Marshal Bill Bouwens, the local one-man police force, hustling into a truck, with the help of some colonists, what could only be the problem worker. The man's arms were tightly bound with cord.

"What are you doing?" Albrecht, unsettled by the sight, asked Bouwens. "This man is ill. Where are you taking him?"

"To Anchorage, Doc. Where he belongs," was the answer. "He's been nothing but trouble, he's crazy as a loon."

"To the railroad hospital?" Albrecht asked.

"Hell, no," Bouwens told him. "To jail. That's what they do with nuts up here." And off went the truck to the railroad station to await the arrival of the train.

Albrecht stared in astonishment at the departing vehicle, swirling up a cloud of dust. Jail? For someone mentally ill? It was impossible in 1935, he thought. He vowed to get to Anchorage as soon as possible and learn what care was given to Alaska's psychotics.

Dr. Romig gave him the cruel facts.

"The law is that persons who are charged with being insane are thrown in jail to await a jury trial," Romig told him. "The jury consists of six residents, none of whom must have medical training. Sometimes a medical diagnosis is made but not necessarily.

"If the jury finds the person is insane, he or she is returned to jail to await transfer to Morningside Hospital, an institution in Portland, Oregon. It's had the contract to care for Alaska's mentally ill since 1904," Romig said. "Young children get the same treatment, even though their problem may be mental retardation or epilepsy or cerebral palsy. If the jury finds them insane, they're sent to Oregon."

Albrecht found the system appalling, particularly since he was incapable of changing it. When he took over responsibilities as commissioner, repeal of the abhorrent treatment was high on his list. As soon as he had tuberculosis under reasonable control, he turned to the matter of Alaska's mentally ill.

In 1949, after he besieged the Department of the Interior with ominous reports on the fate of the mentally ill in Alaska, it appointed a commission headed by Dr. Winfred Overholzer of St. Elizabeth's Hospital in Washington, D. C., to see just how bad things were in the territory.

One witness who gave the investigators a candid account was William B. Healy, a deputy U.S. marshal for Alaska's Third Judicial Division. Marshals were assigned to shepherd the mentally ill to the Oregon institution.

Healy detailed the jury process and added a further dismal note. Transporting the sick individual was yet another travesty, he said, since the person was treated like a criminal, placed in a straightjacket for the trip, finally delivered to Seattle and then juggled on the train to Morningside. Air transportation to Morningside normally took only two days but Healy pointed out that airlines could refuse to carry insane passengers so other and longer routes sometimes had to be used. It was not unusual to confine the person in jail for weeks until there were several patients to take to Morningside, he said.

The commission held public hearings in Juneau, Sitka, Palmer, Anchorage, Nome, and Fairbanks before deciding that "The present commitment procedures for the insane in Alaska should have changed long ago," calling them cruel, inhumane, archaic, and barbaric. It recommended that a long-range program for the patients be initiated immediately and follow a three-part plan.

It proposed first that a modern mental hospital be built in Alaska, then that a fifty-bed treatment center be established at Sitka, and that the territorial government take over and operate the completed facilities. It was precisely the blueprint Albrecht had sought.

The Overholzer committee had not reckoned with the powers at Morningside, however. The Coe family, operators of the institution, was not about to surrender its Alaska contract, and vehemently opposed the Overholzer plan. Alaska's population doubled between 1940 and 1950, and Morningside's population grew proportionately. In that decade, 654 mentally ill Alaskans were sent to Morningside, and federal appropriations for their care more than doubled from $208,840 in 1940 to $534,900 in 1950. Clearly, institutionalizing Alaska's mental patients was a profitable business.

Albrecht knew he was in for a fight on this one, but he was never afraid of opposition, using either patience to await its retreat or courage to face it in battle. In this case, he would need both strengths and more if he were to succeed in establishing mental health treatment within the territory. It would involve a discouraging number of years and ugly confrontations with the Coes.

It was just such personal assets of patience and courage that prompted Gruening to cast Albrecht in another role during this time, this one a distinct departure from his duties as health commissioner. The governor had noted Albrecht's tenacity in pursuing a goal, his quickness in separating wheat from the chaff in complex issues, and his ability to placate antagonists. He liked the fact that his friend shrugged off criticism. Gruening had just the job for someone with those qualities. He would nominate him to be a regent of the University of Alaska.

It was an exceptional honor, one openly coveted in Alaska, as Albrecht was well aware. But he accepted Gruening's proposal from a wellspring few would have suspected.

His Moravian heritage, the one that had impelled him to serve Alaska's Natives, also had a little-known and ages-old veneration for education. In fact, a seventeenth-century predecessor, John Amos Comenius, is considered by the teaching profession to be the "father of public education." When the Moravians settled in Pennsylvania in 1740 they provided instruction through the upper grades for females as well as males. Gruening's proposal was decidedly pertinent; Albrecht had a reverence for education in his bones.

Albrecht arrived on the Fairbanks campus in 1948 at a time of uneasiness among the regents. The eight-member board was split into two factions—four members comprising what was known as the Old Guard, mainly old-timers from Fairbanks, and four known as the Young Regents, all of whom had been appointed by Gruening. Gruening had also appointed one of the Old Guard, Mike J. Walsh of Nome, an ally of the Fairbanks contingent.

The controversy between the two sectors was a matter of educational politics: Should instruction be confined to the Fairbanks campus as it had been in the past (the Old Guard's view), or should the program be extended to embrace needs and interests of other parts of the territory (the Young Regents' view).

Albrecht sided unquestionably with the Young Regents. Like them, he felt the university could be better than it was, should shed its sterile parochialism, must look ahead to the time when extension programs could be established in major Alaskan communities. The Old Guard wanted nothing changed.

The conflict was manifested in the fate of UA's president, Dr. Charles E. Bunnell. Bunnell had a narrow perspective of the university and a firm hold on his office, despite failing health that limited his work. The Young Regents wanted him out, feeling little would advance under his regime. In May 1948, a secret deal was made whereby Bunnell would resign but the resignation would not be announced until October 1948.

Albrecht came on board that October. The Old Guard was dragging its feet on seeking a successor to Bunnell but finally agreed to initiate a search after Governor Gruening approved a memorial from the Alaska House of Representatives that called for the appointment of a new university president "at the earliest possible moment." Albrecht not only introduced the motion for the long-delayed search at the board's meeting on March 9, 1949, but was widely believed to be the author of the memorial.

The hunt led the regents to Terris Moore, a self-employed financial consultant, product of an Ivy League education and Boston Brahmin culture and a familiar figure in Alaska, especially as a mountaineer. Moore was the choice of the Young Regents.

Also in the running was John C. Reed, a well-liked and noted geologist with wide scientific experience in Alaska but no academic teaching background. That failing did not trouble the Old Guard, who made it clear that Reed was their man.

Albrecht met with Moore at the Willard Hotel in Washington, D.C., and came away convinced he was the person for the position.

For his part, Moore said Albrecht "seemed to be pursuing all the right questions. It gave me a feeling of confidence and optimism." Moore added he hoped the other regents "were to be like Albrecht."

The regents met May 12, 1949, to deal with a busy agenda that included a vote for a new president. A number of topics occupied the regents until Albrecht decided they could procrastinate no longer. "Let us deal with the issue that faces us," he asked. "We all know we must choose a new president." But their fortitude did not match his, and the discussion was postponed until after commencement the following Monday.

It was not until May 17 that the regents tackled the election, fearing the four-four split would be a public embarrassment and decide nothing . But the Old Guard solidarity crumbled unexpectedly. The one woman on the board, Harriet Hess, wife of a Fairbanks banker and a board member who had never strayed from the conservative fold, voted for Moore. The startled, accusing stares of her Old Guard counterparts turned from her to Albrecht. Had it been his persuasive endorsement of Moore that had won her vote? If so, not a whit of triumph showed on Albrecht's face. He was simply relieved Moore had been chosen.

Bunnell, however, having been named president emeritus, did not bid farewell. Efforts to persuade him to vacate the administration building failed repeatedly, causing Albrecht to lament, "In retrospect, the situation that developed and was tolerated was that a retiring president continued to have influence by his presence. We—the regents—made a mistake by allowing him to have his office and his residence. Now, this seems illogical and unreasonable."

Albrecht wearied of such infighting, particularly when he envisioned momentous roles for the university. He was especially interested in developing its Geophysical Institute since it was to sponsor arctic research, a growing interest for him. The struggle to acquire federal funding and support for the institute consumed much of the regents' attention. Finally, on July 1, 1949, the building's cornerstone was laid on the Fairbanks campus.

Albrecht was also excited about the Arctic Health Research Center, which was proposed for the campus. At his first meeting as a regent, in fact, the board had donated land adjacent to the university for the project. The center, under the aegis of the U.S. Public Health Service, would study all the areas that concerned Albrecht's department, including environmental sanitation, bacteriology, parasitology, and nutrition. It would be an exceptional resource.

The university's generosity died a regrettable death, however, when the center learned it had no funds for construction. Instead, it was located in an existing building in Anchorage. Later, it was transferred to the UA campus in Fairbanks where it operated until federal money ceased in 1972.

Meanwhile, Albrecht found himself immersed in

eventful change at the university. Having weathered the tense election of a new president, he plunged into a profusion of academic matters—an extensive classroom building program, additional dormitories, increased faculty salaries, summer school sessions, a graduate school, adult education classes and, unexpectedly, the establishment of off-campus instruction.

When this latter issue was placed on the board's table, the regents were taken unawares. It arose when one Rev. P. Gordon Gould let it be known that the Methodist Church was interested in building a private college in Alaska. For the first time, the University of Alaska faced the threat of competition for the few undergraduate students in the territory. Now university officials pondered how to deal with Gould's proposal.

Moore was staunchly in favor of community colleges for Alaska as part of the university system and felt they were the answer to Gould's challenge. However, as a newcomer he was cautious in introducing the idea. The regents were divided on the notion and totally flustered. Albrecht provided them with time to counteract Gould's intentions by calling for a study on the "advisability of establishing branches of the University throughout Alaska." He added that until completion of the survey no action could be taken, which saved UA from an immediate commitment while giving Gould notice the university well might expand.

In time, UA did establish branches in other communities, but it was a difficult and long process. Moore and Albrecht, determined advocates, were bolstered in 1950 by the arrival on the board of Elmer E. Rasmuson, the territory's foremost banker and a resident of Anchorage. Largely through the backing of the three, the legislature in 1951 passed the "Community College Act of the Territory of Alaska" and provided an appropriation of $2,241,000 for the program. In 1953, the university began offering a full schedule of courses at Elmendorf Air Force Base in Anchorage, and the University of Alaska was forever changed.

"This was a period of considerable transition and expansion in many ways for the university," Rasmuson said later, "and Earl was essential in making it go smoothly. We were a good working group. He was territorial-minded and he helped the other regents to think in those terms. He had a long-range view of things, a great regard for the human side. I think that came partly from being a medical doctor and partly because he had been trained in the Moravian ministry."

And partly, no doubt, because he knew the worth of education.

# CHAPTER 10
# Under Siege

*Albrecht probably posed for this portrait during his years as territorial health commissioner.*

Albrecht's star was in ascendancy in the early 1950s. His success in finding and treating tuberculosis, combined with the arrival of new and powerful drugs, had resulted in a remarkable drop in deaths from the disease. He had acquired more hospital beds for TB than the territory had ever had—568 in 1952, and the number would increase with the opening of the Native hospital in Anchorage the following year.

His mastery in cajoling dollars out of legislative bodies and charitable foundations was legendary. In his ten years

in Juneau Albrecht had snowballed the department's funding to $1.4 million per biennium.

In 1949, through impassioned speeches before congressional committees and his letter-writing campaigns, he had
helped win the passage of a $70 million public works pro-
gram for Alaska. At the time, Albrecht called it "the most
important, practical, specific means by which we can improve health conditions in the territory."

The bill provided $11 million for hospitals and health
centers, and nearly $20 million in waste disposal and water
supply systems. Albrecht had told Congress "there are fifty-
eight communities in Alaska of two hundred or more
population and none of the fifty-eight have satisfactory
waste-disposal facilities." Public water supplies were hardly
better, he said, and 78 percent of the beds in Alaska's
fourteen general hospitals were declared unacceptable
because of the condition of the buildings.

The twenty-three existing health centers were also a
disgrace, Albrecht stated. Some had no running water or
toilet facilities, others were in abandoned ANS buildings.
Unless such conditions were corrected, the "haphazard
growth of the territory with its concomitant risks to health,
safety and comfort will continue as before," he warned.

Now, as President Truman signed the bill, the federal
public works program would satisfy his wish list. Nearly
half of the appropriation—more than $30,000,000—would
be used to improve Alaskans' health. Albrecht intended
the bulk of the money to go to the construction of new
health centers, which he considered crucial for people in
the Bush.

Nationally, the reports of the American Medical Association and the Parran Team had added considerable luster
to his reputation. Both had endorsed Albrecht's requests
for increased federal aid, had shamed the Department of
the Interior into upgrading its sustenance of Alaska, and

had been reflected in the public works bill. Albrecht's standing with the federal government and in public health circles
was high and somewhat mighty.

Lois Jund, who as administrative director was close to
the scene, recalls that at that time, "Earl was flying high,
wide and handsome." Jund had become become administrative director in 1948. After heading up the health and
TB education program for two years and finding little effi-
ciency in the main office, she told Albrecht one day what
he needed was an administrator.

"Fine," was the reply. "Draw me up a job description."

When Jund showed him the job description she had
written, Albrecht nodded in agreement, smiled his fabled
smile, and said, "Great. You've got the job."

"And I actually took it and for no more in pay, although
I well knew it entailed much more work," Jund said.

By then, she recalled, "Earl was getting what he wanted,
and although he was getting it for the sake of public health
and making tremendous strides in improvements, there
were those who just bitterly resented him."

Trouble was afoot. Despite, or perhaps because of, his
growing power, Albrecht had become a thorn in the flesh
of a number of people. His independent style of running
his department, his aggressiveness in acquiring funding
and recognition, and his enviable success in achieving his
ends had created strong resentment and opposition within
the Alaska legislature and within his own profession.

He was not unaware of this, but he recognized much of
the hostility had political roots. He had told Gruening in
1945 he would not operate by the standards of the Juneau
hierarchy. He would not exchange favors with legislators,
nor would he have any part of hiring or promoting through
favoritism. He would simply carry out his department's
duties as effectively as possible.

There was grumbling in Juneau. Some legislators

questioned why Albrecht always came away from appropriations sessions with his requests granted when legislators were less fortunate in securing funds for projects and constituents in their home districts.

Some members of his own medical community became critics, too. It was rumored in Juneau that the commissioner was shifting major portions of the health services to Anchorage, which was growing in population. There was speculation he would like to base the entire department there. The hearsay fueled the sharp rivalry existing between the two cities.

A conflict developed in 1952 when Albrecht fired Dr. Grace Field, head of his Division of Maternal and Child Health, citing "loyalty and personality clashes." Albrecht also dismissed Field's husband, J. Frank Field, who had been assistant director of the Division of Sanitation and Engineering, saying he was reorganizing the division.

These three elements—envious politicians, suspicious physicians, discharged staff—prompted the Alaska Legislative Examination and Investigations Committee to conduct an inquiry into the health department. The public hearings opened on September 20, 1954, with Rep. Herald Stringer of Anchorage presiding. Juneau newspapers daily played the story on their front pages.

The proceedings bore a stronger resemblance to comedy than to a courtroom. Testimony frequently wavered between dim recollections and fuzzy pettiness. Reporters covering the hearing had a hard time putting a plausible lead on their stories and determining where the investigation was headed.

Dr. Field was the first to testify at the hearing. She complained of being ignored by the department's Anchorage branch. Anchorage, she said, did not inform her of activities, failed to consult her on pertinent matters, and did not properly delegate authority to her. It was a charge sure to find sympathy in Juneau.

Jund says Field must have suffered from memory loss. "She claimed never to have seen certain reports but there they were with her initials right on them," Jund said.

Field told the committee the disloyalty charge apparently was based on "something I was supposed to have said that I am not aware of to someone who was not designated in an Alaskan town, first reported to be Palmer but later said to be Anchorage."

As for the personality clash, Field said she thought it had to do with differences of opinion in administrative policy. She also said insufficient personnel caused delays in x-ray readings, sometimes for as long as a year. Her husband, in his turn on the witness stand, acknowledged in milder testimony that there had been no delay in sanitation improvements.

The following day, Sen. Marcus Jensen of Douglas testified that a former member of the health board, Mrs. Joseph Kehoe, told him she believed Albrecht's board meetings were too brief. Minutes were often as late as six months in being sent to the board, Jensen quoted her as saying.

Jensen had a gripe of his own. Albrecht, he said, had written to the federal Bureau of Public Roads about the construction of a stretch of the Glacier Highway between Auke Bay and Tee Harbor, calling the roadway impassable. Why, the legislator asked, could not Albrecht have contacted the bureau's district office in Juneau rather than "going to the extent of embarrassing a federal agency that is trying to do something for the community?"

The rambling, disjointed testimony continued for five days and heard, among other things, pros and cons concerning the floating clinics. The debate centered on the use of boats versus planes with the legislators pumping for more airborne service. The skipper of the Presbyterian mission boat *Prentice Hall*, E. B. Nelson, defended the marine units, stating he "didn't want to be in the crew that has to wrestle even just x-ray equipment from an airplane at a place like Angoon."

Nelson also said people in Southeast Alaska were fearful the investigating committee was "knocking the props out from under the health boat system." This caused Sen. Howard Lyng, a committee member, to shake his finger at Nelson and declare, "I resent you, sir, and I want you to know it."

William Paul, speaking for the Alaska Native Brotherhood, endorsed the marine clinics, saying, "At first I thought them a sort of picnic parties where favored persons would be given staterooms and captivating nurses and sent out to have a good time in the villages," but he stated he had become convinced, through observation, that the medical staff was serious about giving people excellent health care.

So went the hearing. A variety of issues, many seemingly irrelevant, surfaced without order and obvious purpose. Lois Jund, for example, was called to defend her insistence on equal pay for equal work, a principle she said Albrecht shared.

Committee counsel William Moran zeroed in on Jund heartlessly, insisting the sanitarians deserved higher wages.

"I couldn't see the point of this or the reason for his arrogance," Jund said. She also resented the legislator who came drunk to the hearings one night and proceeded to lambaste the department health staff.

Albrecht took the stand on September 23 for ten straight hours of testimony. In a calm and steady voice, he addressed the list of complaints and defined Field's disloyalty as attacks on the department and on himself personally, as reported by staff members.

Much of Moran's questioning centered on the budget of the marine units. When he called for per-patient cost statistics, he aroused a rare belligerent reaction from Albrecht.

"There are too many variables, too many different services rendered. You cannot measure health in dollars and cents," Albrecht retorted angrily.

When Moran asked whether Albrecht had written a letter for Governor Heintzleman in support of the marine units, Albrecht stated, "I think it is out of order whether I or anyone is writing letters for the governor." He followed the protest by saying he had never written a letter for the governor nor did he know of such a letter.

Then Albrecht made a request that surprised the committee. He asked for a closed-door session whereby he would give further testimony and name names. "I don't want this to be public," he said, "because what I have to say can ruin some reputations. And even though these are reputations of people who have accused me unjustly, I do not want to embarrass them."

His secret testimony ended the investigation. As it closed the books on the affair, the committee lamely noted it had authority only to make recommendations. It made one—that the marine units be discontinued in favor of planes. Albrecht, under no obligation to accept the proposal, would ignore it.

The following day, the Juneau newspaper, *Independent*, in an indignant editorial, called the proceedings "a depressing spectacle."

It stated the committee "has been too busy trying to settle old grudges and to make political capital for the clique that ran the 1953 legislature to do anything useful or constructive.

"There was the testimony by disgruntled former employees who had been dismissed from the agency. There was the smart-aleck counsel who seemed to think the hearing was some kind of show which had been arranged to display his wit and brilliance. There was the loaded question, the insistence of yes-or-no answers, the refusal of witnesses to really explain the matters about which they were led through lines of questioning prepared in advance." And so on.

"There were some other things," the editorial noted. "A painful evening session at which one of the committee members arrived late, in his cups and full of foggy zeal to question and abuse witnesses; the member from Ketchikan who checked in for one day, collected his per diem and checked right out again; the $100-per-day 'consultant and investigator' who proved to be the highest-paid tape recording machine jockey in the history of the communications industry."

The editorial concluded by saying, "Our territory deserves better at the hands of her elected legislators than this."

Albrecht, meanwhile, sailed through the episode as though it had been nothing more than just another week's work. Jund pointed out that when Albrecht next approached the legislature for appropriations, he was given even more than he requested. "One of the senators said, 'Earl could fall into a pile of manure and come out smelling like a rose,'" she reported.

The brouhaha was scarcely forgotten, however, when Dr. William Whitehead, a physician in private practice, announced, perhaps out of frustration over the folly of the legislative investigation, that he would fire a verbal and public broadside at Albrecht at the monthly luncheon of the Chamber of Commerce at the Baranof Hotel on January 6, 1955.

The prospect of fireworks attracted even those whose chamber membership had lapsed. On the day of the luncheon the Baranof dining room was filled with more than one hundred Juneau residents, eager for the show. The question in the air was whether Albrecht would be present. He was known to have been stranded in Annette the previous evening when fog prevented his plane from landing at the capital's airport. But even before the first course was served, he appeared, imperturbable and smiling.

Whitehead's accusation was a familiar one. Albrecht, he said, was trying to move the health department out of Juneau, to either Anchorage or Palmer. He already had transferred the chronic-disease unit to Anchorage, although he was denying responsibility for having done so, Whitehead said.

"This is the capital and this is where these offices should stay," Whitehead asserted, adding that the constant discussion of moving the capital "somewhere else" was hindering the city's growth.

Whitehead's charge that the commissioner was "not a public health-trained man" had no effect on Albrecht, who was always forthright about his medical background, nor did the criticism of health department budgeting disturb him. But the barb that bit was Whitehead's description of Albrecht as "one who tells untruths."

It was an insult Albrecht believed was so undeserved he could not readily see how to answer it. He feared his emotions, which were known to lead him to tears, would betray him as a weakling. As he struggled with a reply, he remembered a tenet of his father: Truth is the strongest ally.

He ignored the charge of liar and instead explained that the move of the chronic-disease unit was ordered by the U.S. Department of Welfare's Children's Bureau which largely funded the unit. Then he produced letters from the Board of Health stating the board had never discussed moving the department nor had the commissioner ever suggested it. Albrecht made his case quickly and briefly, ending with an offer that caught the crowd by surprise.

"If the Alaska State Medical Association or the Board of Health wants me to resign, I will resign," he said.

Albrecht was safe on both fronts. His board was far too proud of him to consider such an offer, and it would have been an aberration for the medical association to oust him. He was largely responsible for its existence. He had worked in his early days in office to form the organization and bring physicians together.

"One of the things I learned was that the areas of the territory were very distinct—Anchorage, Fairbanks, Ketchikan, Juneau, Nome—but particularly in medicine," he said later.

Establishing the Alaska State Medical Association was "very worthwhile because we strengthened each other with annual meetings, correspondence, contacts."

Unquestionably, the entire censure stung. It was eased somewhat by a long, compassionate letter from Gruening that not only lamented Whitehead's "public excoriation" but also commiserated with Albrecht over the legislature's "inquisition."

"Of course you must know, by this time, if you did not know it fully earlier, that public service subjects those who enter it to misinterpretations, harassment and abuse," his revered mentor wrote. "But the only thing that matters is one's conscience. This is what we have to live with."

Gruening quoted, somewhat inaccurately, Rudyard Kipling's poem "If" and then told Albrecht, "Your head should be both unbloodied and unbowed. You've done a magnificent job with the means at your disposal and the magnitude of the task after three-quarters of a century of inaction, neglect and indifference. You have made Alaskans health conscious. You have built up a great instrument to combat and rout ill-health in Alaska. You have both pioneered and carried the task to where real, permanent, tangible achievement is in sight."

The tangible achievement Albrecht had in sight at the moment was one for which he and many others had labored persistently for years: The transfer of health care for Alaskan Natives from the BIA to the U.S. Public Health Service. It was a highly sensitive matter, bound in politics, pride, and power. But it was also one that could not be set aside. Criticism of the BIA had been mounting for years.

At the heart of it was the medical profession's view that the BIA was not a health organization, that its priorities were education and land management. Criticism of the agency centered on several issues: Its track record in attacking disease in Alaska was seen as less than impressive; it had always had such a difficult time staffing its clinics and hospitals that they were unable to handle their patient load; it was insensitive to the wishes and customs of the Natives; it lacked emphasis on preventive medicine, preferring to concentrate on treatment, which it dispensed in ways better applicable to the Lower 48. Such were the charges.

In fairness, a large part of the BIA's problems stemmed from inadequate budgeting by the Department of the Interior. It was a handicap Albrecht could well understand. In Alaska, the agency was known as Alaska Native Service and it worked with the territorial Department of Health on many fronts. But Albrecht and the U.S. Public Health Service were far more productive in developing health and sanitation programs in the villages. Albrecht also had been far more successful in securing funding. In their common interest of public health, ANS and the health department nevertheless frequently shared responsibilities, such as treatment at the sanatoriums.

This was not always amicable. Dr. Philip H. Moore in Sitka particularly chafed under the arrangement and

penned laments to Albrecht, wondering how to work pro-
ductively with the ANS office at his hospital and thinking
perhaps he did not care to. He was the chief orthopedic
surgeon at the hospital but the administrator was an ANS
appointee, generating a tug-of-war over their respective
areas. Moore confided to Albrecht he was so fearful of
changes being made if he was absent from the hospital
that he probably would miss the 1952 hunting season.

Moore had strong support for his complaints. Margot
Hopping, president of the Alaska Crippled Children's Association, a major supporter of the hospital, released for
publication a bluntly worded resolution.

"Whereas the ACCA is very greatly interested in the
health and welfare of the peoples of Alaska and inasmuch
as it has come to our attention that there is grave danger of
interruption of the continued medical care and rehabilitation program (at Mount Edgecumbe Hospital) and whereas
we have already lost one thoracic surgeon and are fearful
of losing our orthopedic surgeon, we hereby affirm faith
in the orthopedic program at Mount Edgecumbe under the
supervision of Dr. Philip Moore, chief orthopedic surgeon,
and in the Commissioner of Health, Dr. C. Earl Albrecht,
and furthermore we strongly support the move to thoroughly investigate the Bureau of Indian Affairs and the
Alaska Native Service," the statement read.

The news release listed people to write to in Washington, D.C., and Juneau, expressing support of Moore and
Albrecht and urging the investigation "not only as it af-
fects our orthopedic program but in every aspect as (the
BIA) operations involve the general welfare of all the people
of the Territory."

The failings of the shared system were depressingly
clear, not only to those who had to deal with it but also to
visiting experts. A leading recommendation of the
influential Parran Team after its first visit was that

"resources of the Alaska Native Service and the Territorial Department of Health be pooled and placed under a single administration."

In August 1954 Congress authorized transferring Native health services from the BIA to the U.S. Public Health Service, but the federal government looked to Alaska to help with the costs. When Dr. Leonard A. Scheele, the surgeon general, put the idea to Governor Heintzleman in January 19955 the governor responded that the matter needed study.

Heintzleman pointedly informed Scheele, "Natives are normally considered to be the responsibility of the federal government, since they are generally on federal land and not subject to local taxation." At any rate, the governor declared, Alaska could not provide Native health care without aid.

The momentum for change was nationwide and on the rise, stemming chiefly from concerns of Native Americans in the Lower 48. In Alaska, Albrecht had propounded the move for years and, in customary fashion, had exhorted others to join the cause by writing letters and making phone calls to Washington, D.C. His limited department could not attend to all the needs in the widespread Bush, he argued. The consensus was that the territory desperately needed a more effective Native federal health program.

On July 1, 1955, health care of American Natives was transferred from the BIA to the newly created Division of Indian Health of the U.S. Public Health Service. The enabling law stated, in part, "all functions, responsibilities, authorities and duties of the Bureau of Indian Affairs relating to the maintenance and operation of hospital and health facilities for Indians, and the conservation of the health of Indians shall be administered by the Surgeon General of the United States Public Health Service."

This relieved the Department of the Interior of

responsibility for the public health and medical problems
of Alaska Natives and placed it in the new Alaska Native
Health Service office in Juneau. The Interior Department
remained the overseers of Alaska as a territory, however.

The Parran Team's report was issued on the eve of the
transition and pointed out that the new responsibilities
assumed by the U.S. Public Health Service would require
considerable coordination "if the Natives are to be well
served and our tax dollars economically expended." Despite whatever challenges lay ahead, Albrecht viewed the
change hopefully and gratefully.

Another tangible achievement in sight for Albrecht was
legislation pending in Congress providing for care of
Alaska's mentally ill at home. With TB on the wane, he
was able to campaign strenuously for the bill, which was
one of his top priorities. As the measure worked its way
through committees in 1955, he pleaded in Washington,
D.C., for its passage and coaxed others to do the same.

Sen. Bob Bartlett had become a resolute fighter for the
cause, bombarding Albrecht with reports of his lobbying
in the capital and asking for information, advice, and support. It would be a battle to get the legislation passed,
Bartlett warned, but he declared his conviction that, after
nearly a decade since he had introduced his own unsuccessful bill, victory would soon come.

The commissioner could look justifiably, then, at the
forthcoming year, 1956, as one where his most important
hopes for Alaska would come of age. Even his adversaries
conceded he had reached incredible goals in the territory
and in a remarkably brief period.

He might have basked in his glories, treated himself to
a sunny vacation. Instead, on January 6, 1956, he submitted to his board his resignation as commissioner of health
for the Territory of Alaska. He was leaving, he said, to
work for the state of Ohio.

# CHAPTER 11

# Moving On

*Albrecht (left) was acting director of mental
health and correction when this Ohio
groundbreaking took place.*

Alaskans were stunned by the announcement of Albrecht's resignation. Gruening called it a tragedy for Alaska and bemoaned that Eisenhower's administration had "undone much of what had been accomplished in the territory."

"Of course, your leaving Alaska is a great blow," Gruening wrote. "Your accomplishments stand like a great monument." He urged Albrecht to retain his Alaska voting residence, to finish his term on the university's Board of Regents and to be open to returning.

Governor Heintzleman, noting that he found the news

"difficult to believe," stated Albrecht had been "closely identified with everything which represents progress in Alaska's public health program." He, too, held out hope Albrecht would return and that "we will benefit from the knowledge and experience you gain in Ohio."

What was most perplexing about the decision was the timing. The commissioner had overcome his enemies, had achieved status and funding for his department, had built an exemplary staff despite great odds, was on the brink of reaching his cherished goal of mental health care at home, and still had time left in his contract. Why now? the public wondered.

The questions multiplied as his forthcoming title became known. He would be assistant director in the Department of Mental Hygiene and Correction for the state of Ohio. His colleagues were baffled. "It's hardly equal to the kind of authority and position he's had in running Alaska's whole health effort," one of them said. "What can C. Earl be thinking?"

Albrecht's thoughts on the matter remained strictly private. "It is time for me to go," he said. "I've been here more than ten years. The assignment in Ohio will give me the opportunity to learn more about mental health, and that could be of benefit to Alaska as it moves ahead to provide care within the territory for its mentally ill." He had little more to say.

His statement was widely read to mean Albrecht entertained hopes of coming back to Alaska, perhaps not as commissioner of health but in some capacity to deal with mental health. And it was true a future in Alaska was in his plans. He had confided in a letter to Senator Bartlett that he "may desire to return to the territory." Many of the farewell tributes indicated it would be a viable possibility.

Some thought Gruening's departure from Juneau left

Albrecht feeling rudderless. Gruening had been elected as a designee to the U.S. Senate and in April 1953 had left Alaska for Washington, D.C., to campaign for statehood.

There was also the rumor Alaska fell short of Blanche Albrecht's standards for their children's education. In fact, before the opening of the fall semester in September 1955, she had moved with the children to Philadelphia where she enrolled them in school. Albrecht had settled them all into an apartment there, and had spent time at a Philadelphia hospital, being checked for a hyperthyroid problem. He was concerned about his health because he had not been feeling well. Some wondered if this influenced his decision.

Dr. Phillips, chief orthopedic surgeon at the Mount Edgecumbe Hospital in Sitka, believed the stress of working with ANS was Albrecht's chief reason for leaving.

"As long as health administration is divided, the job of commissioner will be almost intolerable," he wrote Albrecht. "How you have survived and accomplished so much in spite of the roadblocks thrown up by people will always be perceived as a near miracle to me."

Senator Bartlett wrote: "Because of your missionary zeal, because of your willingness to fight for sick human beings, people are alive today who otherwise would not be. Perhaps even more importantly, thousands will be restored to full health who otherwise would have suffered years of agonizing sickness. And perhaps even more importantly, other thousands will never become sick, thanks to the programs you instituted."

The University of Alaska was dismayed it might lose Albrecht as a regent. Dr. Ernest N. Patty, then president, urged him to stay on the board, and the regents' secretary, Helen Eyinck, assured him he was "one of the most important and best members." Albrecht, too, said he hoped he could continue as regent, even though he was an Ohio resident, another indication he saw himself back in Alaska eventually.

Atwood's *Anchorage Daily Times* was upbeat about the news. The publisher rejoiced that "in its search for leadership, Ohio has found an Alaskan is the most qualified and able person for the job." It was a rare occurrence, Atwood noted. "The tables have been turned," he wrote. "Instead of Alaska looking to the states for leaders, the state has looked to Alaska and found one." He called Albrecht's new appointment "a singular distinction" that was "accompanied by the gratification that Dr. Albrecht has announced his intentions to return." Actually, there was no such formal public statement, but Albrecht had shared his plans with his friend.

The January announcement was no surprise to the members of the health board. Albrecht had informed them in December of his intent, hoping he could keep it quiet until the board's January meeting. When the news broke publicly, the board was ready with a lengthy resolution fervently extolling their chief's professional record, listing his outstanding accomplishments, and leaving the door wide open for a new appointment later.

Dr. Charles R. Hayman, deputy commissioner of health, was named to complete Albrecht's unexpired term of two years. Albrecht, then fifty, said he would leave office February 1, 1956, but transferring authority turned out to be a thornier task than he expected. It was February 14 before he arrived in Columbus, in a downpour. His family would join him later, after the children's school term was over.

Atwood's pleasure in Albrecht's "singular distinction" was an accurate interpretation on the new appointment. It was a far more weighty position than its title implied. For although Albrecht was leaving behind a $70 million public works appropriation, the Ohio department he would be serving had just received $150 million from the legislature for construction of sorely needed facilities. He would have a critical role in spending it.

Ohio had awakened lately to the miserable state of its mental institutions and to the disgraceful overcrowding of its prisons. It also was beginning to realize its laxity in addressing juvenile delinquency. The $150 million was intended to correct the defects, and, the legislature added, the sooner the better.

Albrecht would share responsibilities for the eighteen mental hospitals and the three state schools for the retarded comprising the Division of Mental Hygiene; for the five penal institutions and their farms and honor camps in the Division of Correction; and for the two industrial schools and diagnostic centers in the Division of Juvenile Research, Classification and Training.

His specific duties were chief of the executive division of the Department of Mental Hygiene and Correction and supervising manager of the hospitals, prisons, and juvenile facilities. As such, he would be accountable mainly for medical administration and development of policy. His salary would be $18,000.

Albrecht believed many exciting undertakings awaited him as he moved to Columbus, but what heartened him the most was he would be working with Dr. John D. Porterfield, the department director. Porterfield had made a distinguished name for himself in his agency, which had been created only a few years earlier out of the Department of Welfare. Public health officials around the nation gave Porterfield high marks as he shaped his new bureau. Albrecht told intimates, "Porterfield being the director was the largest single factor that helped me decide in favor of coming to this position."

Porterfield was equally gracious. Albrecht, he told the Ohio press, had been chosen "in the belief that the assistant director should not be too restricted a specialist but rather should be well-experienced in the general fields of institutional management and medical care."

Porterfield had been running his department without an assistant and was anxious to put Albrecht to work. There was much to do. In the past year alone, more than ten thousand new patients had been admitted to the state's mental institutions. Ohio's prisons had been inadequate for thirty years, and some of the buildings were more than a century old. The public, having approved the bond issue of $150 million, now expected noticeable progress.

Albrecht began with plans for a new reformatory budgeted at $11.6 million and a children's psychiatric hospital to cost $1.7 million. Awaiting his further attention were a medium-security institution for teenage boys and a hospital for mentally ill patients with tuberculosis.

His staff learned quickly that the man from Alaska had his own style. They were astonished to find him visiting institutional campuses to discuss office and laboratory layouts, space requirements, even types of lighting and flooring with social workers, psychologists, recreational supervisors. Once he had these professionals thinking about their needs and work habits, he brought in the architects.

A long-range plan was essential for the extensive construction program, and Albrecht took time fashioning it with the help of authorities qualified in their particular disciplines. For this he reached to experts from all over the country—superintendents of prisons, chief psychiatrists at children's centers, professors in criminology, consultants to mental hospitals, architects experienced in institutional design. They joined specialists within his department in a series of conferences, which Albrecht said "will give us assurance that our buildings will have the minimum of error and the maximum recognition of meeting the needs of people."

Blueprints were only a part of Albrecht's concerns. A more familiar quandary was the shortage of well-trained staff in every facet of the department. He had taken a look at the demographics of Ohio and was alarmed. The state's population was growing and with it came more mental-health problems. The numbers of elderly who would need institutional care were increasing, and crime was on the rise. And Ohio simply did not have enough qualified workers in place for the challenge.

Albrecht was not experienced in prison management, but he could recognize overcrowding. He also knew having one parole officer for one hundred parolees was not good rehabilitation. And he was unhappy with some of the methods used in treating juveniles. He doubted whether $150 million would fix the situation.

Despite his workload, Albrecht took the time to continue his fight for the Alaska mental health bill then under consideration in Congress. He was on the phone and at the typewriter urging passage of the legislation. Senator Bartlett was in constant touch with him. When Governor Heintzleman told the Juneau Chamber of Commerce in July that the territory might maintain a contract with Morningside for as long as ten years for incurables, Bartlett told Albrecht, "I don't think you would have said that!"

The plight of the mentally ill Alaskans in Morningside had become an emotional national issue, intensified by an indignant press. Among its most striking developments was that two Oregon legislators had been inspired to campaign strenuously on Alaska's behalf, even though doing so seriously jeopardized their political careers at home.

On February 10, 1955, Oregon Sen. Richard L. Neuberger had introduced a bill providing for the construction of a 350-bed mental hospital somewhere in Alaska, a fifty-bed emergency mental-health clinic in Southeast Alaska, and the gradual transfer of mental-health care to the territory. At the time, he said he expected substantial opposition within his own state from "local pork-barrel 'I-want-my-cut-too' interests."

No one fought harder for passage of the legislation than Rep. Edith Green of Oregon at the risk of losing support from her voters.

The *Fairbanks Daily News-Miner* pointed out editorially that Alaska had been helpless in the campaign because it had "no voting representative in Congress to lead a battle to change this vicious practice of jailing the mentally ill." Alaskans, it added, "extend a vote of appreciation to the people of Oregon for sending Edith Green to Congress."

Oregon did not welcome the efforts of Neuberger and Green. Morningside was an established Portland institution and a reliable employer. Wayne W. Coe, owner of Morningside, which was operated by The Sanitarium Company, immediately opposed the bill, saying it would mean "the end of Morningside." Almost as soon as Neuberger introduced his measure, the matter turned nasty.

Shortly after the legislation was presented, Bartlett wired Albrecht that the "Campaign launched against Alaska Mental Health Act by extreme elements is in full swing and vigor. Altogether frightening. Anti-Semitism and everything else mixed up in it."

The target of the anti-Semitism apparently was Dr. Winfred Overholzer, who had been sent by the Department of the Interior in 1949 to investigate Albrecht's account of the appalling treatment of Alaska's mentally ill. Overholzer, however, was not Jewish.

The charges, which emanated from the Minutewomen of California and the Hoyas Syndicate of Santa Ana, also in California, claimed the mental health act, H.R. 6376, was a Marxist plot born in the United Nations. The bill provided a grant of one million acres in Alaska to finance operation of mental-health facilities in the territory. The land would be used as a site to imprison conservatives, anti-Communists, and other rightists, the propaganda stated. Albrecht later wrote Bartlett, "The hate campaign was one of the most unbelievable events under the democratic system of government."

Meanwhile, Wayne Coe and his son Henry, general manager of The Sanitarium Company, lobbied medical societies for endorsements and won some. The Coes claimed Morningside had "an excellent treatment program" and a "happy, homelike atmosphere." They fired off a blistering retort to the *News-Miner*, which on June 15 and 20, 1955, ran definitive articles on the controversy.

The Coes saved their heaviest ammunition for Rep. Edith Green, who won a battle to have a financial statement on Morningside included in hearings on the bill. Despite Wayne Coe's earlier insistence that profits amounted to a little more than $24,000 a year, Green's report showed the institution had made a profit of $671,696 in the years from 1936 to 1953—an average of about $37,300 a year. The *News-Miner* put the figure at $1,115,196.

Green also stated the elder Coe collected a salary of $70,000 although he claimed he earned only $27,000. He called the information culled from the financial report "utterly false and malicious." The federal General Accounting Office, reporting to the House Interim Committee, further charged Coe with billing his company for foreign travel and wages of domestics and gardeners at his home. The GAO also asserted that "remains of deceased patients are not interred decently."

When Green persuaded the House territories subcommittee to conduct an audit of the facility—its first in fifty years, since the Coes had resisted all previous requests—the Coes must have known they had lost the

battle. The audit was conducted by Dr. Henry C.
Schumacher, consultant to the U.S. Public Health Service,
and Mary E. Corcoran, a senior nurse officer and psychiatric
nursing consultant for the National Institute of Mental
Health. It drew a picture of a mental health institution right
out of the nineteenth century.

Schumacher and Corcoran found no medical superintendent in charge, one psychiatrist and one physician on
duty two days a week for 344 patients, one graduate nurse
for those in shock therapy, one registered occupational
therapist, one registered nurse for each forty patients, one
part-time school teacher. For night calls, Morningside re-
lied on medical students.

Retarded children were housed with adult patients, and
three infants lived with their mothers in the female ward.
An internist came only once a month to check on the TB
patients, who lived in a room described as "poorly lighted
and furnished with very poor bed space." The dining room
was said to be "exceedingly poor," there was no nutrition-
ist, nor were menus available to learn what the patients
were fed.

Outmoded fire buckets, dangerous to patients, hung
on the walls. There was no pharmacist and no means for
doing x-rays or laboratory work. There was no social worker
to help cured patients return home, with the result that
more than half stayed as long as ten years. Alaska Bush
residents, whose families could hardly afford to visit or
prove their capability to care for their relatives, could spend
their remaining years in the institution. This was fully acceptable to the Coes. The *News-Miner* reported that the
federal government paid Morningside $184 a month for
each Alaska patient.

Added to this was the worrisome information that the
fire marshal had not inspected the buildings for five years
and the institution was unlicensed because of violations of

the local plumbing code. Publication of the audit dealt Morningside's Alaska contract a fatal blow and sent the mental-health bill sailing through Congress.

In brief, the legislation gradually transferred responsibility and authority for the treatment of mentally ill Alaskans from the federal government to the territory over ten years. The act stipulated assistance would be given to provide necessary facilities and to modernize procedures.

The measure required the Alaska legislature to appropriate funds for the administration of its responsibilities and authorized substantial sums to be available to the U. S. surgeon general for the purpose of making allotments to Alaska. Then it created a land grant "not to exceed one million acres from the public lands of the United States in Alaska," to assist in "placing the program on a firm long-term basis."

This latter provision would create legal tangles for Alaska in later years, but with its passage the act was hailed not only in Alaska but throughout much of the sympathetic nation. As President Eisenhower signed it into law on July 24, 1956, Bartlett remarked laconically, "This act has had a tortured and tortuous career."

In Ohio, Albrecht rejoiced. Congratulatory letters flooded his mail, and the phone rang with ecstatic calls. It would be six years before Alaska, by then a state, would have the Alaska Psychiatric Institute in Anchorage, but the change had been approved along with sufficient funding. The fifty-eight-year-old nightmare for the mentally ill of Alaska was ending.

Happy though he was with the outcome of the battle, Albrecht believed he still had to come to the territory's aid in two other crucial matters: construction of health centers and enactment of statehood. The public works program for construction of the centers throughout the territory was lagging. Albrecht was frustrated and concerned by not being on hand to jump-start it. Once again he wrote letters and contacted authorities but he was, he lamented, too far from the scene.

He had better luck promoting statehood. His connections with U.S. senators and representatives were valuable to the cause, and he did not hesitate to use them. Gruening was ever insistent that Albrecht carry his weight in the campaign and also offered a strong recommendation that, as a regent, Albrecht persuade the University of Alaska to confer an honorary degree on Rep. Edith Green, which the university did in 1956.

Meanwhile, however, Governor Heintzleman had written Albrecht a blunt letter in the summer of 1956 urging him to resign from the Board of Regents, admitting that he wanted to install a Ketchikan supporter in Albrecht's place. An Ohio resident had no standing as a regent, the governor claimed.

The letter distressed Albrecht. He had been a faithful and hard-working regent, and the position epitomized his hopes of returning to Alaska. What should I do? he asked UA President Ernest N. Patty.

"I don't know why your absence should diminish your value as a regent," Patty wrote. "You are one of the outstanding members of the board and I have leaned very heavily on you for advice in many matters which affect the territory. That is one reason I was so sorry to see you leave Alaska."

Patty was not optimistic about Albrecht's chances, however. He noted that although Heintzleman "is aware of the many contributions you have made to the University as a regent, he has it firmly fixed in his mind that you should retire in favor of someone physically residing in the territory."

Both Albrecht and Patty feared pressing the issue would create a "difficult situation," but the matter was resolved when the territorial legislature ruled that anyone serving on an Alaska commission must reside in the territory. By that time, Heintzleman was out of office, replaced by Gov. Mike Stepovich.

Albrecht sadly submitted his resignation June 10, 1957. The regents immediately drafted a resolution stating, in part, that Albrecht "made outstanding contributions aiding the development of the long-range program for the university, especially in the fields of physical expansion, research, student aids, public health and the humanities," and it paid tribute to his "unusual devotion to the University of Alaska."

Albrecht's residency had also caused a stir in Ohio. Shortly after he arrived in February 1956, the state auditor, James A. Rhodes, challenged Albrecht's appointment, saying he had not lived the necessary year in Ohio to be an elector, as required. The accusation surfaced from time to time and was finally silenced the following February when Albrecht, having been in Ohio a year, met the requirement.

However, the complaint was a warning to Albrecht. A vendetta was brewing in Ohio politics and against the mental health department in particular. Albrecht might have given it some mind had not destiny once again revised his path and claimed his attention.

On October 16, 1956, Porterfield called Albrecht into his office, smilingly asked him to have a seat, and then gave him staggering news: Porterfield was leaving Ohio to become an assistant to the U.S. surgeon general. Porterfield and Gov. Frank J. Lausche wanted Albrecht to step up as director of the Department of Mental Hygiene and Correction.

Albrecht was stunned. He had been on the job eight months. He was immersed in an enormous building program, far larger than any he had ever handled. He was instituting vital changes in the department's divisions. It seemed unlikely he could take on additional responsibilities. And most troubling of all was the departure of Porterfield, a major reason for his taking the Ohio position. Now Albrecht felt stranded.

"Give me some time to think about it," he asked Porterfield, but even as he said it he knew the change would be painful and the decision difficult.

# CHAPTER 12
# Ohio Challenges

*Ohio Gov. O'Neill (left), Albrecht (in front passenger seat) and others tour Ohio's mental health and correction facilities.*

D r. Porterfield's unforeseen farewell and the offer of a promotion to the directorship jolted Albrecht, even as it intrigued him. It would be a natural role for him. He was in the habit of being in charge. But he liked his assignment. He was exhilarated by his commission to build new facilities and to modernize old ones for the Department of Mental Hygiene and Correction. He had shaped the plans; now he wanted to see them carried out.

Further, there was more appeal to his job than bricks and mortar. He was learning ways to treat the mentally ill and mentally retarded, to rehabilitate prisoners, to head off juvenile delinquency before it ruined a young person's life. He had come to Ohio, he reminded himself, for just such an education and he did not want to sacrifice it to administrative duties.

Porterfield, he had noticed, was overworked. Albrecht did not fancy the extra hours additional responsibility would demand. Blanche and the children had joined him in Ohio after their school term ended. Jane was sixteen and Jack twelve, and Albrecht wanted to spend more time with his children. Virginia, who had joined the Albrecht family during the war, was grown, married, the mother of two, and living in Seattle.

There was also a disquieting aspect of the director's position, and that was Ohio's entrenched political warfare. It was unlike what he had found in Alaska. The intense and historic rivalry of Republicans versus Democrats permeated state government, and the Department of Mental Hygiene and Correction suffered a disagreeable share of it.

Alaska had given Albrecht a taste of this rivalry, but it was daily fare in Ohio. Worse yet was the vehemence of the state's press. Newspapers in the major cities were fiercely partisan and used not only their editorial columns but often their news space to press their political views on their readers.

The *Columbus Citizen*, a Scripps-Howard evening newspaper in the state capital, had its sights trained on Governor Lausche's Democratic administration. The Mental Hygiene and Correction Department was a favorite target of one of its columnists, James T. Keenan. A Lausche appointment, Porterfield was a frequent Keenan victim, as Porterfield hinted to Albrecht while he was still in Alaska.

After his secretary had typed a welcoming letter dated January 28, 1956, Porterfield had added a hand-written note. He told his new assistant that his publicity had been good and Atwood's laudatory *Anchorage Daily Times* editorial had been quoted in the Columbus morning paper.

"However," he wrote, "there is one newspaper in Ohio which is presently trying to wring this department out. They haven't hit you yet and doubt they will. For what?"

Keenan was on Albrecht's trail. The month Albrecht arrived in Columbus, Keenan addressed a letter to the University of Alaska Board of Regents, inquiring whether Albrecht had severed connections with the board or was still a member. The letter eventually found its way to President Ernest Patty who sent it to Albrecht, expressing puzzlement.

"Why should they be concerned about your connection with the Board of Regents?" he asked Albrecht. "Possibly there is a political curve involved, and I wanted to alert you in advance." Patty advised Keenan to query Governor Heintzleman who, he noted, handled such appointments. Heintzleman then shunted Keenan's request to Dr. Hayman, his new commissioner of health, who answered with a glowing account of Albrecht's Alaska record, skirting the question.

It was during the same month that State Auditor Rhodes raised the issue of Albrecht's residency, a good indication of hatchet jobs to come. The *Citizen's* hostility dampened Albrecht's enthusiasm for Porterfield's job. And Porterfield's salary was no enticement, either. Locked in by statute, the position paid only $12,000. Albrecht's salary was $18,000. No wonder Porterfield jumped at the surgeon general's offer, Albrecht thought.

So his answer to the director and the governor was a courteous thanks but no thanks. He would stay on as acting director, he said, until a successor for Porterfield was found. Then they could decide on his role.

Meanwhile, buildings were to be built, programs managed, funding sought, and reports written. Lausche ran for the U.S. Senate, relinquishing his governorship. In November 1956, Ohio elected C. William O'Neill, formerly the attorney general, as its new governor. Almost immediately, Keenan, the newspaper columnist, wrote that the mental hygiene department, which he called "inefficient and antiquated," was due for revamping when the new governor took office.

Most of the criticism was directed at Porterfield for not getting projects off paper sooner, but it was now Albrecht's job to bypass the controversy and get on with the work. He proclaimed the spring of 1957 would see the "biggest building boom ever of state public buildings." Coming were a $7 million reformatory, a children's psychiatric hospital, medical and surgical units for two mental hospitals, and $6 million in additional improvements.

Less than three months after stepping in for Porterfield, Albrecht could report substantial gains on three fronts—mental hygiene, adult correction, and juvenile rehabilitation. For the first time, Ohio's mental patient load had been reduced, despite the ten thousand-plus influx, because of improved treatment, new drugs, and better community placement methods. A new 120-bed building for the insane was going up.

The construction of the Marion Correctional Institution would result in less crowding, and a penal institution due for Warren County made the prognosis brighter yet. Nevertheless, Albrecht emphasized that many more improvements were needed.

Better diagnosis, classification, and treatment were helping juveniles, and the new diagnostic center would be a further bonus. For the first time, schools for juveniles had full-time physicians on staff.

"We need a new approach for young people," Albrecht said. "Rather than just send them to industrial schools, let's see if we can find what's the matter and what's best for them. This calls for an individualized approach, with a clinical team to study each case from different viewpoints."

This time Albrecht had a newspaper, the *Cleveland News*, in his cheering section. "The dark shadows are lightening for Ohio's mentally ill," it said editorially. It even credited Lausche, Porterfield, the legislature, and Ohio's voters for the reform and added that "Dr. Albrecht will accelerate this."

However, the honeymoon with the Ohio press was brief. In February 1957, the *Cleveland Plain Dealer* said Porterfield resigned before he proved his fledgling department's worth as an independent agency and it was now drifting. Albrecht was a medical doctor and health administrator, the newspaper said, and O'Neill wanted a "name psychiatrist," adding, "Billy is dragging his feet on the appointment."

The *Columbus Citizen* joined the chorus, again raising the matter of Albrecht's status as an elector (although by this time the former Alaskan had lived the required full year in the state) and speculating about a possible taxpayers' suit.

This was a gentle forerunner of the invective Keenan let loose in March. He added up the millions the legislature had appropriated to the department and then said, "A man of national prominence in the mental-health field" (but naming no names) termed Albrecht's heading of the department "ridiculous."

Keenan zoomed in once more on the elector issue, claimed the department was a year behind in its annual reports, and chided O'Neill for not taking action. When he reported on the investigation of Albrecht by the Alaska legislature, the newspaperman wrote about criticisms against Albrecht but made no mention of his defense.

Making it read like the official record, Keenan wrote, "He talked a good game, the committee said, but was way below par on performance. Too many programs were launched with a fanfare of publicity and then left to wilt on the vine, said the lawmakers." There was no mention of the victory over tuberculosis, of the new health centers, the acquisition of hospitals, the reforms in Native health care, or of any of the other achievements Albrecht left behind in Alaska. Nor could the quotes Keenan used be found in the hearing's transcripts.

Albrecht's reaction to the diatribe was typical—he dismissed it. And, as usual, he laid all his troubles on the altar of his Lord, knowing they would then vanish.

Although he could not escape by fishing as he did in Alaska, he did enjoy his National Guard membership. Since World War II, he had served the guard as surgeon and medical officer and termed it "such a satisfaction." He never missed his required weeks of encampment and looked forward to them like a boy anticipating vacation. He remained active until age 60 when retirement was mandatory.

He also concentrated on his work, pleading before Ohio lawmakers for more funds. The legislators either missed the media attack or discounted it, for they voted to add $1,700,000 to his department's budget.

He was adamant in his requests. The juvenile division was overcrowded, but he could not make use of its empty cottages because he had no staff for them. An improved family-care program needed funding so mental patients could go home earlier. Prisons needed more and better-trained and better-paid personnel. Opportunities for professional advancement and increased salaries would attract more proficient employees and enhance recruitment.

Albrecht's message to the legislature was this: Buildings alone are not the answer. He warned that Ohio's prison population had hit an all-time high of more than eleven thousand and would continue to rise, even with completion of the new Southern Ohio Reformatory at Lebanon.

"To attempt only to build new institutions in a race to

keep up with this rapidly growing prison population would be wrong both morally and economically," he said.

In answer, he sharply increased probation and parole programs throughout the counties and proposed a medical facility for sex deviates, alcoholic offenders, and others needing specialized treatment. He also called on the private sector for help, urging "a massive effort, primarily at the community level, to strike at the causes of crime."

Albrecht struggled along with judges of juvenile courts to set up systems to determine which young offenders needed more intensive residential study and treatment. He was anxious to bring more juveniles into professional rehabilitation channels, and did so with the new 150-bed Juvenile Diagnostic Center at Columbus State School, an institution primarily for the retarded.

As foundations were laid for Ohio's mammoth building program, Albrecht also lobbied for new personnel. Less than a year after becoming acting director, he was able to report that the number of physicians serving full-time in Ohio's hospitals for the mentally ill had risen 34 percent.

"The ratio has dropped from one physician to 144 patients a year ago, to one to 110 today," he reported. "It has been the awakening of public awareness in recent years of the vast problem of mental illness, resulting in increased financial support of the mental health program, that has made this gain possible."

Albrecht carried the load of supervising the multimillion dollar construction outlay as well as overseeing all operations of the mental and penal institutions, and this without an assistant. He headed a department that employed 12,687 people and was responsible for the welfare of 47,578 state wards. Yet the press was dissatisfied, pressuring O'Neill to name a director for the department.

On September 23, 1957, the governor reached deep into the department's administration and came up with the name of Dr. Robert A. Haines, a superintendent at one of the state's mental institutions. Although he was a nine-year veteran of Ohio's mental hygiene division, Haines was hardly the "name psychiatrist" the *Cleveland Plain Dealer* had expected to head the agency.

When reporters asked O'Neill where this left Albrecht, the governor replied, "The question of what happens to Dr. Albrecht will have to be decided by him and Dr. Haines."

Dr. Haines made a quick decision on the matter: Albrecht was out. In fact, Haines was so intent to evict Albrecht from his post without delay that he prematurely issued a press release two days later, on September 25, 1957, stating Albrecht had been fired. That same day however, hours earlier, Albrecht had sent Haines his resignation, which had been requested. Department records showed his resignation as voluntary. It was effective Nov. 1, 1957.

Albrecht told Haines he would like to retain his Civil Service status as physician specialist and remain in the department in some capacity. Haines' response was to assign him to Columbus State School at a $2,000 reduction in pay, and a lowering of his professional standing.

It was a devastating turn of events for Albrecht. Months later, in a letter to Lausche supporting statehood for Alaska, he referred to that day as "one tragic morning in September."

For consolation, he had the editorial in the *Akron Beacon Journal* which stated, "As his reward for almost a year's service as acting director of the Department of Mental Hygiene and Correction, working most of the time under conditions which only an extremely patient man would have tolerated, Dr. C. Earl Albrecht has been fired.

"If, as may logically be suspected, the ouster of Dr. Albrecht was ordered by Governor O'Neill or one of his

political advisers, Dr. Haines himself is in trouble," the
editorial continued. "Dr. Albrecht's biggest handicaps as
acting director during the O'Neill regime were the uncer-
tainty of his status and a lack of contact with the Governor's
office."

The *Beacon Journal* reported that when asked about the
situation, Albrecht said, "I have endeavored to find out
why such drastic action should be taken and I could find
no reason. I had indicated to Dr. Haines in writing and to
the Governor and to others that my desire was to remain
with the department and work with Dr. Haines and anyone Dr. Haines would like to bring in. However, this was
not acceptable and I was requested to resign immediately."

"The treatment accorded Dr. Albrecht seems quite un-
fair," the newspaper editorialized. "The abilities, training
and experience which he combines are too valuable to be
thrown away."

Asking why Albrecht was fired, the editorial went on,
"We can only guess. He has scrupulously avoided political
activity. When asked what the Legislature did for Mental
Hygiene and Correction, he would state the facts precisely
as he saw them. Not that he went around the state com-
plaining. He simply refrained from claiming that the record
was better than it really was."

Albrecht had lived by his father's motto that truth was
the strongest ally, the motto that had sustained him in
Juneau during Whitehead's attack. In Ohio's political climate, however, truth had been a liability.

Albrecht, the former acting director of the Department
of Mental Hygiene and Correction, did, indeed, accept the
position at Columbus State as physician specialist—and
later said the experience gave him "a deeper understanding
of the problems of the whole care for the retarded." But he
was not there long.

In October 1957, he was asked by Dr. Charles L. Wilbar,

secretary of health for the Commonwealth of Pennsylvania, if he would be interested in coming to work for him as deputy secretary of health.

Albrecht was overjoyed at the thought of working in what he called "my own state, next to Alaska." As word of his dismissal filtered through the nation's public health offices, the state of Tennessee had offered him a high-ranking health position. But Pennsylvania, which had courted him quietly for years, was his first choice. In December, he accepted the new position. His last day of employment in Ohio would be January 14, 1958.

Albrecht was saddened by the circumstances of his departure from Ohio, but he was not bitter. As he wrote Lausche, "Working with you and Dr. Porterfield was one of the most satisfying periods of my professional career." He had learned much in Ohio.

Now he arrived in Pennsylvania, where he was welcomed with open arms. His mother lived in Bethlehem, his daughter had been accepted at Moravian College, and Moravian pulpits throughout the state sought his sermons. Dr. James A. Crabtree, head of the department of public health practice at the University of Pittsburgh School of Public Health and a member of the Parran Team, signed him on as a lecturer, which raised his state salary to $18,000.

Gruening, his faithful friend, wrote from Washington, D.C., to wish him well. "My delight is tempered only by the fact that your new job isn't in Alaska, and that you are not back there again, serving in the admirable and unforgettable way in which you served for so many years to Alaska's lasting benefit."

Albrecht had hardly settled into his Harrisburg office when he heard from Solly Hart, his convict chauffeur, about the sorry state of affairs in Albrecht's old Ohio department. Hart, once called Cleveland's Public Enemy No. 1, had drawn a life term for the gangland-style murder of Roy

"Happy" Marino, an ex-convict who had won a suspiciously early release from prison and was slated to tell the attorney general how he became so fortunate. Marino was killed before he could enlighten the attorney general. During imprisonment, Hart had endeared himself to important people, including his warden and Lausche, who reduced his sentence to 20 years for manslaughter.

Hart was a free man when he wrote Albrecht, although an aching one. Warden R. W. Alvis had insisted on taking the wheel one day when Hart was his driver, landing both of them in traction following a serious accident. With a numbed hand and wearing a steel brace, Hart was taking a respite from driving but had time to reflect on Ohio politics.

"After you left I didn't do much driving for the mental health department any more," he wrote Albrecht. "I went to the warden and asked if I can't give it up, he asked me why and I told him the truth, I said I don't care to drive them any more, my heart's not in it and I can't drive anyone or be sincere about my work."

Hart was apparently a practiced judge of character, from the warden ("he gave the cons faith and hope and he was my friend") to O'Neill ("I told you he would be a one-term governor") to Keenan ("he couldn't understand why so many nice people would go to bat for me") to Dr. Haines ("he asked for my address but he never came to see me the four months I was in the hospital").

To Albrecht, he wrote, "I can't forget the days and nights Doctor Porterfield and yourself worked so hard. Every day and every night, you were exhausted. Governor O'Neill came into office and took credit for what you and Dr. Porterfield did. For that reason I turned down a job working for the State of Ohio, I couldn't forget the deal they gave you."

Senator Lausche also lamented Albrecht's experience.

"The treatment which they (the O'Neill administration) accorded Dr. Porterfield and yourself was wholly indefensible," he said in a letter to Albrecht in Harrisburg. "They labored under the belief that success would accompany them if they promptly labeled everything which I and my associates did as wrong."

Albrecht also heard from Dr. Harry V. Gibson, Alaska's new commissioner of health, but on another matter. Gibson told him the new system for bringing Alaska's mental patients home from Morningside was working well.

The discharge rate was being stepped up and a mental health clinic had opened in Anchorage. Architects were working on plans for a major new facility to open within a few years.

Dr. Philip Moore had pleaded that mental patients be sent to his Mount Edgecumbe Hospital, noting that because tuberculosis had been conquered, many beds were available. However, Anchorage was chosen as the site for the Alaska Psychiatric Institute, which was completed in 1962.

Albrecht could not quarrel with that decision. He recognized Anchorage as the center of Alaska's population growth and was grateful the long struggle for local care of Alaska's mentally ill was over. There remained the quest for statehood and even as he began his duties in Pennsylvania he wrote members of Congress seeking support. Albrecht's heart was still in the north.

# CHAPTER 13

# Pennsylvania Beckons

*The University of Alaska awarded Albrecht*
*an honorary degree in 1964.*

T he Earl Albrecht who returned to Pennsylvania in 1958 was far different from the Earl Albrecht who had left it in 1935. Now, at age fifty-two, he had been forged by years in the nation's severest climate, in an unfamiliar culture, in assignments that demanded (and got) his total strength and all of his talents, in the center of ruthless politics—all taking him from one-room cabins in rural Alaska to the halls of Congress. The process had broadened him.

Yet there was much that was the same about the man. He still believed in his sacred calling to serve his fellow

humans through healing, he still renounced the machina-
tions of governmental power cliques, he still spent more
hours on the job than he ever counted, and he still loved
to fish.

After wading through the congratulatory letters and
telegrams, Albrecht began to size up the health needs in
Pennsylvania. He was heartened by the firm grip Secretary
Wilbar seemed to have on his office. Yet both he and Wilbar
could see problems.

Albrecht had learned in Alaska that the best care be-
gins at home. In Pennsylvania, some communities lacked
adequate health services, and many counties had no boards
of health. Yet this was hardly the last frontier.

"What I saw was the health of Pennsylvanians was average but, for me, that was not good enough," Albrecht
said. "Too many counties in the commonwealth were not
taking advantage of the opportunity to secure state financial aid to finance health programs on the county and local
level. Funds that should have been going to them were
being used for health services in other areas that were organized."

As he had many times before, Albrecht turned to state
legislators for help. He believed Pennsylvania should have
public health services in every county with a population of
at least one hundred thousand and multicounty local health
units for the smaller counties. Local taxes would pay for
one-third of the cost, and the state would pick up the rest.

In the 1950s, many Pennsylvania counties still operated under antiquated governmental systems that did not
adapt easily to change. Albrecht saw he would have to go
county by county—"from Easton to Erie," as he put it—to
motivate constituencies for creation of local health departments. He looked to chambers of commerce, service clubs,
the League of Women Voters, local newspapers, and other

civic organizations to carry his message to county and state officials.

Shrewdly, Albrecht focused on issues that affected the general public. One he raised successfully was the lax state regulations on milk that resulted, he said, in "a major source of the spread of intestinal diseases." He urged that supervision of milk processing and distribution be transferred from the state Agriculture Department to the Health Department.

Faulty sewage disposal, he warned, was responsible for a growing number of cases of hepatitis. He urged county commissioners to support septic tank legislation to halt pollution caused by sewage infiltration of drinking water. Grant money was available for communities that acted quickly.

Albrecht's views were underscored by a year-long study of Pennsylvania's health needs completed by the Johns Hopkins University School of Hygiene and Public Health in 1961. Three municipalities—Allentown, Bethlehem, and Erie—harkened to Albrecht's urgent appeal, using a Local District Law that provided for joint city health departments. But for many communities the law did not allow that option. Albrecht was constantly on the stump for the passage of Senate Bill 703, which would correct the deficiency.

Pennsylvania's entrenched and vast industrial economy caught his attention as well, and he was troubled by some flagrant safety loopholes. He worked with drug companies on a code of regulations adopted on September 1,1961. Until his legislation was enacted, the government did not oversee drug and cosmetic manufacture in the state. "People could make the products in their bathtub, if they chose," Albrecht said.

The code's mediating teams—meeting nights, weekends, and Sundays—praised Albrecht for his "enormous contribution to the passage of the drug code."

One participant, George H. Hafer, wrote him, "You are recognized for not only knowledge, skill and patience but for your integrity." Under Albrecht's leadership, he said, the mediators had considered and agreed upon all the amendments presented by the major prescription drug companies before presentation to the legislature. "We were ready for victory," Albrecht said.

Air quality, particularly in the steel communities of Pittsburgh and Bethlehem, needed improvement, so he developed a laboratory to monitor air pollutants. Carrying documentation of adverse health effects to the state legislature, he led a campaign for an antipollution bill passed November 9, 1961. It was one of the first in the nation.

Community public health was always the bedrock of Albrecht's professional philosophy. He labored to strengthen it in Pennsylvania by linking statewide agencies with voluntary and private health activities. It required forbearance, tact, and the energy of a team of horses. He was constantly on the road, meeting in cities and towns with groups such as United Cerebral Palsy and the Society for Crippled Children and Adults, listening to their concerns, outlining state policy, and offering guidance.

It was a tiresome task, but the efforts promoted greater cooperation among agencies and with the commonwealth. Furthermore, the increasing harmony and support fortified the Department of Health in its requests to the state legislature. It was a bonus Albrecht, with his thorny political history, would not have overlooked.

If Albrecht seemed even busier than usual in 1962, few guessed the reason. His marriage, after years of discontentment and, more recently, separation, ended in a quiet divorce in February. Albrecht filled his days and much of his nights with work in hope of stifling the pain. For a person with such strong religious principles and ingrained traditional values, the divorce was a bitter reality.

However, life was about to get brighter. Dr. Roy Sexton, a friend of Albrecht's, had noticed Albrecht's loneliness. It put him in mind of a young widow, Margery Jones Stancil, whom he knew in Arlington, Virginia. When Albrecht came to the nation's capital on business, Sexton, who lived in Washington, D.C., saw his chance to play matchmaker and artfully arranged a picnic on his boat.

"You always had a great time with Roy Sexton, so when he invited me to join a group for a trip down the Potomac, I was delighted to go," Margery said. "Since we were to leave quite early, I suggested they all come by my house for breakfast. And when I met Earl I thought to myself, 'Why, he's kind of cute!' "

Albrecht, too, was pleasantly surprised. Sexton had not told him he would be meeting a popular and attractive brunette with considerable Southern charm. He asked for her phone number, as casually as possible, and managed to engage her in conversation most of the day. The happy outing was cut short so Earl could catch a plane back to Pennsylvania, but Sexton's matchmaking was progressing nicely.

"As Earl got out of the car at the airport, I turned around to look at him through the back window," Margery said. "Later he told me that when I did that, he knew he had a chance." And he was determined to pursue it. Although Margery had mistakenly given Earl an old phone number, he tracked down her current number and arranged a date.

Margery had no shortage of suitors, but she also had no intention of remarrying soon. Earl, however, had long since discovered the value of persistence. He hastened to Washington from Harrisburg every weekend, arriving at Margery's door with roses and outstretched arms. With his courtly manner—after all, he had been nicknamed "Duke" in college—women had always found him appealing. Now he prayed Margery would too.

His luck held. On May 4, 1963, Earl and Margery were married at Riverside Church in New York City with Sexton the best man. The marriage brought Earl not only the love of his life but also the joy of Margery's daughter, Linda, then twenty-one. They were an instant family, so close that new friends assumed Linda was Earl's natural offspring.

It was a momentous year in another way. In January 1963, Jefferson Medical College offered Albrecht a position, to begin in May, as professor of preventive medicine. He viewed it as a door opening to a whole new world for him. He accepted almost immediately.

Albrecht was no stranger to teaching. While in Ohio he had been an adjunct professor of preventive medicine at Ohio State University. In Pennsylvania, he had been a lecturer in the Department of Public Health Practice at the University of Pittsburgh, and at the Women's Medical College in Philadelphia. At the time of the offer he was a visiting professor of preventive medicine at Jefferson.

He had a natural talent for the art of teaching, some of which must have risen from his Moravian heritage of teaching and healing. He loved the classroom, the ferment of intelligent discourse, the stimulation of diversified ideas. He rejoiced to see bright young people choosing his revered profession, and his uncommon medical experiences reinforced and enlivened his instruction.

The new position meant an uprooting once again. He had enjoyed his time with the Department of Health and well knew that critical issues still confronted the office. But the appeal of Jefferson, his alma mater, was too compelling.

Further, Albrecht chafed under the perversity of the Pennsylvania legislature. To his exasperation, the county health units and a comprehensive state health plan he had advocated died early deaths when Pennsylvania lawmakers balked at the funding. He put the blame on the growing emphasis on expanding the welfare system at the expense of health programs. Although he had made many satisfying improvements in his assignment as deputy secretary of health, he was frustrated by the tug-of-war of power politics. Academia promised a well-deserved change.

Now another outpouring of good wishes, congratulations and plaudits came his way. William E. Graffius, then executive director of the Pennsylvania Health Council, which Albrecht served as president, summed up Albrecht's achievements as deputy secretary of health.

"C. Earl Albrecht is remembered as a public health visionary," Graffius said. "This was a key to his contributions as deputy secretary. The areas of his influence most strongly felt throughout the Commonwealth were his efforts to provide a comprehensive health plan for the state and to establish county health departments. These did not come to fruition but yet they set important standards.

"His work on the community level—igniting interest on the part of the Pennsylvania Medical Auxiliary to highlight health concerns, for example—was very valuable. He was especially effective working with the Health Council and involving the public and private schools.

"Dr. Albrecht was the key to the successful marriage of state government and the voluntary health agencies. He worked with the cancer society and then the state tuberculosis society to originate, promote, and design programs on smoking and health. This put Pennsylvania in a national leadership role, and we see his early influence to this day."

One attraction of the Jefferson appointment was Albrecht would still have a hand in the public domain. Jefferson wanted him not only to teach but also to help head up a projected study, requested by the U.S. Public

Health Service, on neurological and sensory diseases, their treatment and facilities. Jefferson was to research Delaware, southern New Jersey, and the eastern half of Pennsylvania, and the state's Department of Health was to cover the western half of Pennsylvania.

This would bring Albrecht into the lives of those with cerebral vascular disease, head injuries, seizures, cerebral palsy, alcoholism, malnutrition, brain tumors, Parkinsonism, eye and ear problems, and related illnesses.

The project's directors were Dr. Albert L. Chapman for the commonwealth and Albrecht for Jefferson Medical College. They headed teams of forty-five health professionals who for twenty months plowed through records, analyzed and interpreted data, conducted interviews, scrutinized hospital care, visited nursing homes, studied statistics, and evaluated field personnel. Then they drew their conclusions and wrote their recommendations.

The conclusions were hardly glowing. The researchers found that neurological and sensory diseases were affecting tens of thousands and requiring hospital care for more than seventy-five thousand people a year. There was a shortage of personnel trained in the field, particularly surgeons. Basic hospital facilities for diagnosis and treatment were severely inadequate. Albrecht must have felt he was back in Juneau, given the familiar problems.

The study found one out of every ten deaths in the tri-state region was due to neurological disorders. Smaller hospitals rarely had neuro-sensory, board-certified specialists, the survey showed, but specialists were also in short supply in larger hospitals. Distribution was a concern, since city hospitals, especially those affiliated with medical schools in Philadelphia and Pittsburgh, were far better staffed than those in rural or smaller areas.

The ultimate recommendation was the establishment

of a neurological and sensory disease center at Jefferson Medical College. This, the project participants stated, would provide for more well-trained physicians, expanded research, and better diagnosis and laboratory resources. The center would make large numbers of "teaching beds" available to medical students and would offer community education and information programs.

"We're going to need it all," Albrecht said. "People are living longer and these diseases are steadily increasing. As they go untreated and undiagnosed, society must pause and reflect upon its responsibility and give thought to what should be done."

The college laid its case for the center's appropriations before Congress, but committed the blunder of not sending Albrecht to Washington, D.C., to speak for the cause. Perhaps the institution did not know his track record in obtaining funding in the nation's capital. At any rate, the request was turned down, to the chagrin of all who labored over the study.

"It wasn't a total loss," Albrecht said philosophically. "The findings gave us indisputable proof of the needs in the tri-state area, and medical institutions picked up on that. Even without federal money, programs were set up and more attention was directed to the problem."

Albrecht interrupted his work on the neurological and sensory disease study in 1964 for an emotional trip to Alaska. In March, he received a letter from Dr. William R. Wood, president of the University of Alaska, inviting him to participate in the commencement exercises scheduled for May 25.

"On this occasion," Wood wrote, "the University of Alaska would be pleased to confer upon you, in recognition of your distinguished career in medical science and your significant contribution to the development of public health in Alaska, an honorary doctor's degree. All of us in Alaska are particularly mindful of your splendid work in establishing on a firm basis Alaska's public health program, your work in tuberculosis and your success in establishing the Native Hospital in Anchorage."

If Albrecht did not actually know the impetus for the degree he must have had suspicions his friend Ernest Gruening was somehow responsible, and he would have been correct. Gruening, still in the U.S. Senate, wrote in March 1963 to Elmer Rasmuson, then president of the regents, that the tribute was due. Rasmuson agreed.

It was not Albrecht's first such honor. In 1951, his alma mater, Moravian College, had given him an honorary Doctor of Laws, which he cherished. But the Doctor of Science degree from the University of Alaska would have special meaning. As he wrote Wood later, "Without question, the receiving of the honorary degree from the University of Alaska is one of my most abundantly satisfying experiences. Such an honor for my efforts in the earlier days of Alaska's development is deeply appreciated."

Albrecht beamed as he ushered Margery around the campus with its many new buildings. "The physical facilities are utterly remarkable," he told Wood. "I remember so well the difficult time we had to convince some Alaskans many years ago that we must build well and first-class for the future."

Meanwhile, with the neurological study nearing completion, Albrecht answered a plea from an old friend, H. Rex Lee, now governor of American Samoa. Lee had tried to entice Albrecht to Samoa in 1962 with the position of medical director there, and as an inducement he dangled plans for a new hospital and told Albrecht he could have the fun of designing it.

Lee's terms were somewhat vague, however, and before he could get them firmed, Albrecht had received and accepted Jefferson College's offer. Now, in 1964, Lee asked if Albrecht was interested in a short-term assignment as medical consultant to the projected hospital. Lee could pay him the weekly equivalent of $20,000 a year, plus expenses.

Both Albrechts were thrilled with the thought of several weeks in romantic Samoa. The lure of moonlit beaches and exotic tropics proved irresistible. Earl convinced his dean, Dr. William A. Sodeman, that the experience would enhance his lectures in international health.

Margery and Earl spent from late November 1964 to January 3, 1965, at Samoa. As they reveled in the lush surroundings, Albrecht also designed the 158-bed hospital. Lawrence D. Conway, a health-facilities planner who followed through on construction, later wrote Earl, "You did a program which permitted our success after others had failed, and I hail you for it."

On the return trip, Albrecht met with public-health officials in Sydney, Singapore, Bangkok, New Delhi, Calcutta, Teheran, and Karachi. The exciting itinerary had been funded with a gift of $5,000 from Francis Boyer, chief executive officer of the pharmaceutical house, Smith, Kline and French, who asked that it be used to further Albrecht's scholarship. Boyer had come to think highly of Albrecht when he was deputy secretary of health for Pennsylvania. Boyer particularly admired the way Albrecht had handled enforcement of the new drug and cosmetic code.

The neurological study was finished, but Albrecht became involved in other projects. He had become a governor of the Arctic Institute of North America, an international association to promote research in polar areas, and was president of the Pennsylvania Health Council, a coordinating agency for sixty-five health-oriented organizations.

The council gave him a platform to speak for his favorite causes, especially local health units, the need for more health personnel, and increased public funding. He had a standard theme he presented whenever he spoke on health issues: Pennsylvania was failing to match national advances in health care.

"Why is it," he asked, "that Pennsylvania has made progress in commerce, highway construction, the introduction of new industry, and expansion of the old and has expanded civil service coverage, but has never had a 'health year' in legislation?" At sixty, Albrecht was still pressing for the causes he believed in.

# CHAPTER 14

# Northern Mission

*Dr. Frederick Milan played a key role in
establishing a circumpolar health organization.*

By 1966, Earl Albrecht had been absent from Alaska for a decade, but the state was never out of his heart and seldom out of his thoughts. In absentia, he had served his beloved northland faithfully and diligently when he could. Even during his tempestuous Ohio days he had turned from his troubles to push for care within the territory for Alaska's mentally ill, to exhort the territory's public health department to get on with construction of the health centers, and to lobby Congress to grant Alaska its rightful rank as a state.

Albrecht had another goal. This was one of his own,

193

born in Alaska many years earlier in the icy isolation of the
North Slope, in impoverished Native villages riddled with
disease, at his commissioner's desk, wrestling with ways
to get the competent staff he needed. In those days, the
array of obstacles that stood between the people of Alaska
and decent, twentieth-century well-being was overwhelming. It begged for rescue, for remedy.

As commissioner, he had heard the cry and answered
it with compassion and diligence. He had the hard-earned
reward of knowing many iniquities had been corrected since
the auspicious day when the *Hygiene II* took to the waterways. That was substantial satisfaction but not sufficient
to Albrecht, who also knew that, beyond Alaska's borders,
life in communities through all the arctic and subarctic regions was every bit as perilous and difficult as it was in the
Bush he had served.

His love of the north and its peoples had impelled him
to keep close ties with arctic organizations throughout his
public health career. He had learned Alaska's Natives were
not alone in their miseries. As commissioner he had heard
Canadian counterparts recite the woes of their Native population, all painfully familiar to him.

Working with the Arctic Health Research Center and in
his membership as a governor in the Arctic Institute of
North America, Albrecht saw that the brutal conditions
were perpetuated not only in Canada but in Finland,
Greenland, Scandinavia, Iceland, and Lapland as well. He
suspected they also could be found in Siberia and other
northern parts of the Soviet Union.

The missionary in him could not tolerate that; it grated
against his innate respect for God's children. Somehow, he
resolved, the suffering of people in the world's other frigid
regions must get the validity, the respect, the care that was
the right of all human beings. As it had been his goal to

heal distressed Alaskans, so he would find ways to help the people of the entire arctic. Improving the health of people in the northern regions worldwide became his new mission.

Only one with Albrecht's invincible faith could envision the success of such an ambition. After all, he could not even speak the languages of the countries he had in mind. He had no idea where the money for such a venture would be found. Where he would find the knowledgeable saints willing to commit to such an effort was a concern that troubled him not one whit. The demand, he believed, would surmount any such hurdles.

His appointment at Jefferson finally cleared the way for him, after completion of the neurological study, to shift from dreams to action. He had plenty of claims on him, what with preparing lectures, counseling students, and participating in health activities throughout Pennsylvania. But he was no longer a public servant. He had a new and personal freedom.

In the spring of 1966, packing his bags to attend a meeting in Montreal of the Arctic Institute of North America, Earl turned to Margery and said, "I'm going to see what this board of governors will think of my idea for a symposium on circumpolar health. I'm just going to throw the idea out on the table and hope they like it. I've got to start somewhere, and that seems like a reasonable place."

Albrecht had the board's full attention as he laid out the purpose of the symposium. It would provide an opportunity, he said, for scientists, physicians, and health specialists in arctic communities to compare notes on their particular fields, to share solutions for the demands of their unique professional responsibilities. From an exchange of that kind, they could learn what works and what doesn't, he said. It might even build interest in treating arctic Natives and, he reminded the board members, they all knew the scarcity of medicos with that kind of motivation.

The board thought it a fine idea and even appropriated a small sum to get it started. Now, Albrecht was told, raise the necessary money, persuade some institution to host the meeting, set a date that would be widely agreeable, send out information to all likely international participants (and determine who those participants would be), establish a format for the symposium, arrange for accommodations and meals and, oh, yes, don't forget to tape and publish the proceedings.

Quite an order, but Albrecht didn't flinch. He was lucky once again, this time because attending the meeting was Dr. Frederick Milan, a faculty member at the University of Alaska and a human research physiologist with the Arctic Aeromedical Laboratory for the U.S. Air Force in Fairbanks. Milan was a worldwide traveler and an accomplished, perceptive scientist who had fallen in love with the north. He was enthusiastic about the symposium plan, fully recognized its potential. He readily agreed to be Albrecht's cochairman.

Dr. William Wood, president of UA and a strong supporter of scientific arctic research, offered the facilities of the Fairbanks campus. The U.S. Public Health Service contributed $65,000, and the symposium was under way. Invitations went out from lists compiled from a variety of sources and were accepted in gratifying numbers.

On July 23, 1967, delegates from the United States, Canada, Norway, Denmark, Sweden, Greenland, Iceland, Finland—and, despite the constraints of the prevailing Cold War, even one from the Soviet Union—gathered in Fairbanks for what was hailed as the First International Symposium on Circumpolar Health. The planning committee, representing participating countries, had decided all proceedings and subsequent publications would be in English. Other than that, guidelines were few.

The five-day session was a revelation in how little was known about the north. And it revealed a woeful lack of scholarship. Many of the papers presented reflected minimum scientific methodology and narrow application of findings. They tended to concentrate incongruously on demographics, history, geography, and economics.

Yet, there were glimmers of valuable research in pulmonary disease, hepatitis, mental health, tuberculosis, adaptation to cold climates, environmental stress, and zoonoses—diseases that can be transmitted to humans by vertebrate animals. These were all concerns the participants shared and were convincing indications the conferences had a useful future.

"It all proved to be so worthwhile that the Europeans said, 'We must have the next meeting,' "Albrecht recalled. It was agreed similar symposia, subsequently called congresses, would be held every three years, each in a different country. Oulu, Finland, was chosen as the site of the second congress, but it was four years before it took place.

Albrecht immediately sought to confirm a U.S. position in the fledgling organization. With the assistance of Milan and other Americans in attendance, he formed the American Society for Circumpolar Health before the Fairbanks symposium closed. It was an informal body, created to sustain interest in keeping the congresses alive. Now that his dream had been born, Albrecht was determined to see it grow.

At the third congress, held in 1974 at Yellowknife, Northwest Territories, Canada, the alliance emerged full of vigor. It had a new, if still imperfect, maturity. Papers were more professional, areas of study were broadened, data was more precise. By now there was also a spirited camaraderie, spawned of mutual respect, among the veteran members. Through the offices of the Scandinavians, Russian participation increased.

The Yellowknife meeting showed that the myriad old problems of arctic life remained to be discussed and disclosed a few new ones. In a preface to the meeting's proceedings, Dr. Roy J. Shepard, faculty member at the University of Toronto's School of Medicine, noted that although rapid changes had come to the arctic regions, many health problems remained and had not been addressed.

Makeshift housing and sanitation, substandard nutrition and hygiene, diseases, epidemics, and infections all combined with a rugged physical environment kept mortality rates far higher than in southern regions, Shepard said. And as Natives moved from nomadic camps to more modern communities, civilization was a mixed blessing. Alcoholism, suicides, venereal diseases, deteriorating dental health, pollutants, guns, even snowmobiles were taking an alarming toll, he warned.

The fourth congress, in October 1978, was especially rewarding for Albrecht and Milan since they helped organize it under the chairmanship of V. P. Kaznacheyev, an academician with the Soviet Academy of Medical Science and a representative from Siberia. Albrecht had been elated to have Kaznacheyev attend earlier meetings with a few countrymen; now the Russian would be the host at Novosibirsk. Medical science had prevailed over world politics.

If there had been Cold War concerns about the mood of the Russian congress, Kaznacheyev dispelled them with Intourist guides, two-day trips to Lake Baikal, gifts of brandy and candy, and a final banquet where Albrecht, as senior member of the American delegation, managed, through eight rounds of toasts, to convey warm greetings.

"I have looked at Siberia from Alaska and hoped someday to visit, and now the time has come," he told the gathering. "We have met many new friends and we thank you."
Albrecht and Milan, traveling home from the congress,
found themselves with Kaznacheyev on the plane to Mos-
cow, and the acquaintance blossomed into friendship. The
Russian's grasp of circumpolar medicine greatly impressed
Albrecht and strengthened his hopes for further participation by the Communist country.

As the American Society for Circumpolar Health became an official body in 1980, Albrecht was already laying
the foundation for what would become officially the International Union for Circumpolar Health. The brave expec-
tation amazed Dr. John Middaugh, Alaska's state epidemi-
ologist and a founder of ASCH. He had caught up with
Albrecht and his dream when Dr. Helen D. Beirne, in
Albrecht's old job as head of what was now the Alaska
Department of Health and Social Services, named him a
delegate to the fifth symposium at Copenhagen in 1981.

"Before I went to Denmark, I was extremely skeptical of
the whole circumpolar health project," Middaugh says. "It
sounded like just a great boondoggle to go up to Copenhagen.
I expected a lot of work that wouldn't be interpretable. There
was a similarity of problems, but because of money and logistics and trying to communicate with people in other languages and trying to understand different methods of diagnoses and measurement, there didn't seem to be much hope
of getting anything done.

"And this was 1981. But Earl saw, way back in 1967,
that not only was this kind of exchange desperately needed
but that it could work. He and Fred Milan shared the vision to understand at that time the similarity of problems
in the arctic and how important it could be to share experiences and solutions and collaborate with individuals in

other countries who might have far more to contribute than some of us more limited visionaries."

However, when Middaugh went to Copenhagen, where he spoke on rabies control and meningococcal meningitis in Alaska, he did not find the disorder he had anticipated. "When I saw and met colleagues from other countries, I was very impressed that the health problems I had met or been involved with in Alaska were so similar in other countries that affected people of the arctic—various outbreaks of food and water-borne diseases, problems of vaccinating kids, TB still hanging on, injuries, the emergence of chronic disease, the lack of data, infectious diseases, alcohol, the tremendous logistical problem of delivering modern health care in the vast distances and the terrible weather and communications problems."

What Middaugh saw in Copenhagen was the framework that was shaping into a cooperative structure. "Even as I was trying to understand all this," he said, "Earl was working on a constitution and bylaws for just such an organization. At the 1984 congress in Anchorage, he took me and a few other whippersnappers under his wing and transferred his knowledge to us, passing the baton for the responsibility of developing and seeing through the work he had started."

Middaugh was assigned to take Albrecht's constitution and bylaws to the participating nations for approval and signing. "You have to remember that there was no money for travel," Middaugh said. "European countries are better at funding this kind of exchange than is the U.S. In drawing up these formal statements, Earl had to get input through correspondence over time, meeting face to face only every three years with occasionally the opportunity to make a phone call through these time zones. And the tremendous thing was to bring in the Russians. Earl maintained, as did

Fred, these very critical relationships with real persistence."

At their annual meeting in October 1986, ASCH members voiced their eagerness to honor Albrecht and Milan for their efforts and dedication in creating the thriving circumpolar health project. The concept of an endowment fund, which would support American attendance, was approved unanimously. Although there had been some original intent to restrict the tribute to Albrecht alone, Milan's role proved to be too significant to be ignored. Dr. Frank Pauls, also an ASCH founder, suggested incorporating Milan's name into the foundation title. The members agreed and the Albrecht-Milan Foundation was born.

"Milan was a remarkable person in his own right," said Middaugh. "He was a physiologist and anthropologist who had studied at the universities of Oregon, Wisconsin, and Copenhagen, and at the London School of Economics, but his outstanding forte was his love for the north and its people. He was an exceptional scientist who had a warm commitment to the same values Earl Albrecht shared, what I call 'the heart of social justice,' which is public health.

"Fred could speak twenty to thirty languages," Middaugh said, "and lived with Native peoples in Alaska, Canada, and Lapland, learning and speaking the dialects. He and Earl did collaborative studies with the Danes, and through the success of those efforts came the first circumpolar conference.

"Earl, as I understand it, was the visionary, the charismatic, the politician, the recruiter, and Fred was the nuts and bolts, the one who assembled the teams, handled the details, did the science," Middaugh added. "That was how they functioned, pulling together to focus on topics to pursue."

Milan, who died January 28, 1995, left behind a wealth of stories his colleagues treasure. Middaugh remembers a cab ride with him in Sweden when the cab driver "nearly ran us off the road, he was laughing so hard at one of Fred's ribald jokes."

Carl Hild, long involved in arctic Alaska research and work, admired Milan's affection for Natives, and tells how Milan reacted when he reported to an Inupiat senior citizens' group in Barrow on the findings of an ancient site where Natives had died.

"Fred had examined the frozen bodies and concluded that a large ice mass had collapsed on the people," Hild said. "He had all the scientific evidence and answers and was in the process of explaining this to the Natives when he felt a tug on his sleeve. He looked down and here was an Inupiat elder looking at him with kindly patience. The elder said, 'You don't have to tell us how they died. We know how they died. An evil shaman sent the ice flying and that killed them.'

"Milan understood," Hild said. "He simply said, 'I believe you're right,' tossed his scientific notes aside, sat down and had his lunch with the seniors. It was that kind of empathy that endeared him to everyone."

In 1987, the year after the Albrecht-Milan Foundation was formed, Albrecht received what may be the highest award in circumpolar health. At the congress in Umea, Sweden, he was given the IUCH Jack Hildes medal for "humanitarian service to the people of the North and outstanding contribution to the integration, coordination, and promotion of circumpolar health and research in the Arctic and Subarctic." It was the first time the medal, named for a revered Canadian health researcher, was awarded.

By 1987, the symposia had become the International Union for Circumpolar Health. The 1984 meeting had shown readiness for incorporation by attracting 770 scientists and health professionals to Anchorage. The regional office for Europe of the World Health Organization, the body responsible for WHO programs in the arctic, convened working groups at the meeting. Studies of Antarctica were now included in the presentations.

Since then, congresses have been held in Umea, Sweden, in 1987; in Whitehorse, Canada, in 1990; and in Rekjavik, Iceland in 1993. In the years since 1967, more than two thousand papers, most of which have been published in bound editions, have been presented by representatives of twenty-one countries. Anchorage hosted the tenth IUCH congress in May 1996.

As succeeding congresses reported on the growing control of tuberculosis, whooping cough, and measles, they noted previous illnesses had to some extent been replaced by new ones. And although these were less deadly, they were nevertheless debilitating.

Mental illness, addictive behavior, seasonal affective disorder, lung cancer, HIV infection and AIDS, suicide, genetics and human adaptation, problems of adolescents, hearing impairment, smoking, obesity, and fetal alcohol syndrome appeared with escalating frequency as modern concerns. The introduction of modern services like Head Start uncovered other deficiencies such as poor oral health, and, all too often, child abuse.

The overview of arctic life broadened as the meetings progressed to include such social factors as understanding and respecting cultural distinctions, the effects of poverty and poor housing on health, occupational hazards, domestic violence, exploitation of Natives, and institutionalizing the elderly. Clearly, the arctic was undergoing an invasion of urban ills in addition to its traditional ones.

Perspective changed for the scientists. They increasingly sought the cooperation of Natives, inviting them to contribute papers and opinions and to assist in research. Otto Schaefer of Canada admonished the Whitehorse assemblage not to discount the elders' "old wives' tales," which he said have unrecognized value in medicine. Carl Hild, defining the alcohol problem of Barrow, urged the Copenhagen congress to put its faith in the Inupiat community to provide the solution.

Native participation in planning the 1996 meeting was substantial. Albrecht's dream is not only a reality today but has exceeded his hopes by making the people he sought to help now players on the team.

# CHAPTER 15
# Alaska Calls Again

*Earl and Margery Albrecht enjoy a cruise together.*

The success of the International Union for Circumpolar Health seemed to Albrecht to crown his medical career in the north, but Alaska was not through with him yet. Nor was he about to relinquish his bond to the state. Rather, with his summers now free, he and Margery led tours of the state, first for alumni of Moravian College and later for friends from Jefferson. In his usual organized fashion, he designed the itineraries and arranged for all accommodations.

In 1970, following a year as acting chairman of the Department of Preventive Medicine and Community Health,

Albrecht reached retirement age at Jefferson. The college asked him to stay on for an additional year, which he did, but he knew it was time to move on, and he had an enterprising idea where he might go.

For some time Dr. Howard Romig, Dr. Joseph Romig's son, had pleaded with Albrecht to urge his students to consider work in Romig's medical and surgical clinic in Anchorage. "We have to turn away thirty to forty patients every day because we don't have enough staff to handle them," Romig wrote.

Oil had been discovered at Prudhoe Bay on Alaska's North Slope in 1968, and the state was swept up in another tumultuous boom. People were streaming into Alaska to seize the myriad opportunities to get rich quick, get poor quick, and have a rousing time of it in the process. The need for health services, and just about every other human service, exploded almost overnight.

Romig's urgency was fresh in his mind when Albrecht received an offer in 1971 to join the College Medical Center, a private clinic in Anchorage. "Why not?" he asked himself. In the years since leaving the commissioner's office, he had managed to slip back to Alaska frequently but the visits were always too brief. A position at the center would allow him and Margery to enjoy Alaska year-round and revive cherished friendships. They sold their house outside Philadelphia and moved to Anchorage in high anticipation.

Albrecht's name had not long been added to the center's sign before people in Palmer learned of his arrival. Within days the center's waiting room was running out of seating space as Palmer patients demanded to see only "Doc" Albrecht. As much time was spent reminiscing as in medical exams, Albrecht found to his amusement.

At the same time, the University of Alaska put him to work as visiting professor in preventive medicine and public health administration in its WAMI program. A first-year medical school curriculum affiliated with the University of Washington, the program had been established since Alaska lacked a four-year medical school. (Montana and Idaho had similar courses; hence, the acronym was WAMI, for the four states involved.) Later, he became an affiliate professor of medical science at the university.

This meant commuting by plane to the Fairbanks campus in all kinds of weather and taking time off from the clinic. Albrecht often flew to Juneau, as well, to serve voluntarily on the Violent Crimes Commission. His assignment was to help determine whether victims of crimes were entitled to compensation from the state.

After five Alaskan winters in practice at the College Medical Center and teaching at the university, Albrecht, now in his early seventies, developed an appreciation for southern temperatures during the colder months. He and Margery bought a farm near Roanoke, Virginia, "where he could see mountains," according to his wife. But he returned to Alaska each summer as a *locum tenens*, a temporary substitute, so physicians at the center could take vacation leaves.

Although he had sold the log house, he still owned the 150 acres in Palmer he had bought there while running the hospital, and he pondered what to do with it. He chuckled over the unsuccessful flower business he and Bob Atwood tried to establish on the property. When Atwood pointed out that the less they grew, the higher the profits, they decided to shut down the operation entirely. Albrecht tried to interest Gov. Walter J. Hickel in developing the tract but the canny governor suggested he appeal to the Palmer Chamber of Commerce instead.

These were balmy years for Albrecht but with a heavy heart he discerned a festering sore among Alaska's people which he could not dismiss. Daily he read in the newspapers far too many accounts of assaults, accidents, and, often, death due to excessive alcohol consumption. Although the affliction seemed to be prevalent throughout the state, he noticed it was particularly widespread among the Native population. He saw it in his medical practice, and when he talked with village health workers, he heard grim stories of the effects of exorbitant drinking on families and youths. The tales and statistics not only saddened but angered him.

The warning signs had cropped up even in the last stages of his term as commissioner, but alcohol was not then nearly as accessible to the Bush, nor was there the money to pay for it. But the boom had extended to the villages as well, contractors were hiring frantically, and paychecks were fat. Suddenly, there was enough money for booze.

By the 1970s, bootleggers and liquor distributors, with the greater availability of planes, had established a flourishing out-of-town business. Shipments of alcohol could be ordered from city suppliers by phone and delivered to the villages on the next flight. The cost was high but not, apparently, prohibitive.

Commissioner Helen Beirne, also head of the Division of Corrections, saw the devastating effects in the inordinate number of Natives in jail on alcohol-related charges. Knowing Albrecht's prison experience in Ohio, she sought his help. With $10,000 from her budget, she sent him to survey the scene. "As usual, he gave of himself completely," she said.

For three summers, Albrecht traveled Alaska, concentrating on Barrow, Bethel, Kotzebue, Dillingham, Ketchikan, and Nome. He met with physicians and social workers, read police reports, talked to public safety officers and listened to people's opinions and personal accounts. What he learned appalled him.

"I found to my horror that the effect of alcohol abuse was just indescribable," Albrecht said. "It was the single contributing factor to high welfare costs, hepatitis, drunken driving, crime, homicides, suicides, and death. It was not limited to Eskimos and Indians—it was bad everywhere and, worse yet, it had gotten into the schools.

"I'm not anti-alcohol, I'm anti-alcohol abuse," Albrecht stated. "A certain amount that is not going to lead to abuse or ill health is understandable in our society. But when we have free and open bootleggers and our courts don't give them any kind of sentence or punishment, it gets out of hand."

He was heartsick to see the devastation alcohol was causing in his beloved Moravian community of Bethel. It was an example of what was happening in other larger communities in the Bush. Bethel's population then was forty-four hundred, of which more than 95 percent was Native. Its surrounding communities varied in size from thirty to seven hundred inhabitants, totaling 17,502 and including a Native population of fifteen thousand or 88 percent.

With a state Native population of 17 percent, Albrecht was distressed to find it over-represented in alcohol statistics—43 percent of all suicides, 38 percent of homicide victims, 60 percent of alcoholism deaths and an average of 39 percent of all arrests occurred among Natives. Natives comprised 67 percent of all client admissions to state-funded alcohol programs.

It was the entertainment of the Kuskokwim Delta villagers to come to Bethel to shop, visit friends and relatives, and, more than likely, get drunk. The local newspaper, the *Tundra Drums*, had a spirited editor, Rosie Porter, who was not above taking a drink or two but who abhorred what intemperance was doing to her community. Editorially she waged a battle against bootleggers and weak police involvement. She supplied Albrecht with data from her weekly court reports showing alcohol was involved in more than 68 percent of arrests for aggravated assault, domestic violence and other crimes.

The commander of the Bethel post of Alaska State Troopers told Albrecht more than 90 percent of police force work was related to alcohol offenses. Although they spent nearly all their time and efforts on the problem, the police, he admitted, were pitifully ineffective. It was a culture problem, the commander said. Often village police were called upon to arrest a friend or relative. Given the ancestral ethnic bonds of the people, an officer who pressed charges would be ostracized, even by his own family. Furthermore, the police seldom knew how to handle a raging drunk, the commander said. Sometimes they just made things worse.

Albrecht was infuriated when he saw teenagers stumbling in the Bethel streets. Police told him 63 percent of the town's problem drinkers were between the ages of twenty and thirty. Those between the ages of fifteen and thirty-two accounted for 70 percent of the area's suicides and comprised 65 percent of homicide victims. A cab driver told him he stopped driving his cab because it was "too depressing picking up drunken teenagers."

Yet Bethel supposedly was "dry," the result of a 1973 election that closed bars and liquor stores. However, bootlegging was wide open and alcohol readily and easily available for those who had the $40 to spend on a bottle. The question of whether to make alcohol consumption and sale legal was on every Bethel ballot since 1973 but had been defeated, usually by margins as narrow as 1 or 2 percent.

Albrecht himself took out an ad in the *Tundra Drums* for the upcoming election, urging voters to retain the ban. He pointed out that before 1973 there had been 1,615 hospital admissions for injuries, and in 1974, just one year after the ban went into effect, only 144. Many residents thanked him for his support, telling him that even with its bootleggers and scant law enforcement, the town was better with its specious "dry" status.

"I had to take care of the neighbors' kids when the bars were open," one woman told him. "Now the parents are home and the kids don't fall asleep in school so much. People used to drink until the supply was gone. They'd come in from the villages, try to walk home, drown, or freeze. One neighbor always beat up his wife when he got drunk, but she wouldn't turn him in because she needed him to fish."

The entire state, Albrecht announced, was caught in a scourge every bit as insidious as the scourge of tuberculosis he had fought forty years earlier. Alaskans drank twice the amount of alcohol as did people in the Lower 48. The first year of his survey showed 70 percent of fatal automobile accidents involved drinking. Statewide, 55 percent of all crime was alcohol-related, he reported.

"Although the prevalence of problem drinkers cannot be estimated by geographic area, there are indications that the relative impact of alcohol-related behavior is greater in rural-city areas," Albrecht's report stated, referring to the six Bush communities he had visited. "The general death rate, which in Alaska contains a high percentage of alcohol-related causes of death, is actually higher in the less densely populated areas."

His first report went to the state in 1979. In 1980, the legislature issued a policy statement titled "Special Efforts in Response to Alcoholism and Alcohol Abuse Problems." It reflected the lawmakers' concern for the destruction caused by unrestrained drinking. Legislators backed their statement with a prodigious appropriation of $15,870,000 for local alcohol programs.

In a major step the following year, the legislature passed the Alaska Local Option Law which empowered voters to choose the role alcohol would play in their communities. They could elect "dry," whereby the sale, purchase, and consumption would be banned; or "damp," whereby the sale and purchase but not the possession of alcohol would be banned, or "wet," whereby sale, purchase, and possession would be legal.

"The Natives wanted this law," Albrecht said. "By the '70s they had had the experience of years with alcohol, and they saw what it was doing to their people, their children. They wanted to be able to make their own choice, but politics was getting into the issue, liquor dealers were putting pressure on the legislators, and there was always the loud-speaking advocate of self-privilege, personal rights."

The Local Option Law, nevertheless, had enough loopholes to dissatisfy the villagers, who rejected its restrictive election dates and its failure to strengthen law enforcement. In 1982, they won their demands when amendments provided that elections on alcohol could be held at other than the usual voting times (many villagers did not want to wait for the regular election days) and additional enforcement powers were given to troopers and magistrates.

Having already rescued Alaskans—and mainly Native Alaskans—from the curse of tuberculosis, Albrecht, at age seventy-seven, was impelled to throw them a lifeline once more.

His final report to the state in 1982 pleaded for more prevention, in keeping with his medical philosophy. He proposed seven controls, from reducing the accessibility of alcohol by limiting the number of outlets and their hours of operation to raising state liquor taxes to help pay the social costs of alcoholism.

He also advocated picking up intoxicated individuals and placing them in treatment facilities, a practice subsequently instituted by a number of Alaskan communities.

Another Albrecht proposal that has been adopted is increased vigilance in enforcing the prohibition of sales to intoxicated persons.

The former commissioner felt alcohol abuse had gotten out of hand in Alaska when the welfare division was added to his old health department and sanitation removed. It was the same mix he had deplored in Pennsylvania. In Alaska, vital health education was lost, according to Albrecht.

Alaska has a young population, Albrecht said. "We need education in nutrition, alcohol, drug abuse—the whole package of health control that worked for the Natives. It's not being done as a major program in the state. It's a tragedy that it's not a priority and does not have all our agencies and all our knowledge and wisdom applied to it.

"That's what we did with tuberculosis," he adds. "It was an all-out effort by the state, the federal government, the people and the communities to fight it and it could be done with alcohol."

Albrecht went national with the shameful Alaska situation in 1982 with an article in *Nutrition Today*, a health magazine. He outlined how he saw the Natives' particular problem with alcohol, stating that "one must measure the cultural shock they are experiencing as they adjust to the white man's ways—something, by the way, most of them want to do."

He described the Native Alaskan as "kind, caring, sharing, stoical, and considerate," then added, "however, give the drinking Native alcohol and his personality changes. . . . One reason for this transformation in his nature is, I think, that the Natives who drink cannot drink in moderation."

Albrecht traced this to traditional patterns of eating until the food supply was consumed. "Until very recently, even a generation or two ago," he wrote, "and for many not even a generation ago, these people lived as hunter-gath-erers and followed a subsistence economy. On the coast, when they'd get a walrus or a whale, they'd have a feast—they'd eat and eat. The same is true with the inland people—they ate the wild animals and fish, caribou and the like."

It was the same with liquor, he said. "Set a bottle in front of them and they'll drink it until they're intoxicated. And when they awaken they'll continue drinking 'til it is all gone and they may not have another drink for months."

The opinions aroused heated charges of bias, racism, paternalism, and misinformation from some Alaska pro-fessionals involved in alcohol treatment programs, but Com-missioner Beirne defended him.

"Those of us who understand the tremendous amount of energy and effort it takes to continue to fight the major epidemics of the world owe him a vote of thanks for his continued dedication to these causes," she said.

Albrecht's study of Alaska's alcohol troubles depressed him as a bleak denouement of his vocation in the last fron-tier. He thought wistfully of the harried but satisfying days and nights tending to the colonists of the Matanuska Val-ley. How innocent those times were, he reflected, how precious. And, he had to admit, how very long ago.

But three years later the colony years were suddenly back in his life. In July, 1985, at age eighty, he attended the fiftieth anniversary celebration of the Matanuska settle-ment and was besieged by middle-aged people whom, he was informed, he had delivered. Some had their mothers with them, and these he embraced warmly as his eyes filled with tears.

It was Don Gulberg, however, who struck deepest into the doctor's memory. Now a husky, healthy fifty-two-year-old and a long-time Federal Aviation Administration employee, Gulberg strode up to Albrecht and said with a grin, "The one thing I remember about you is that you gave me a Popeye doll. And you know, I've always wondered what happened to it."

Albrecht, on the other hand, had often wondered what had happened to Gulberg. The doctor could not forget the night in 1937 when he received a call to come to the Gulberg farmhouse, some ten miles away, because their four-year-old son, Don, had been badly hurt. Since the Gulbergs had no car, Albrecht used the makeshift ambulance, taking along Max Sherrod, who always feared for his life when the doctor was at the wheel. A fast driver, Albrecht reasoned this was no time to change his habits.

At the house, they found a grisly scene. "The child had been kicked in the forehead by a horse," Albrecht recalls. "His right eyeball had been knocked out of its socket and was dangling on his cheek. His forehead was crushed so that I could see macerated portions of the frontal lobes of his brain.

"God had given him to me alive and I wanted to keep him that way," he continued. "We got him to the hospital and his family could not stomach watching what I was going to do, so they waited outside. All alone, I laid him on the table in my little operating room, gave him a few whiffs of ether now and then as I removed the injured eye, which I knew I couldn't save, dissected the injured portions of his brain, sewed the membranes back together, tied off the bleeding blood vessels, got the bone fragments in place as best I could, pulled down the flap of forehead skin that I had turned up, bandaged him as best I knew how, and carried him into my bedroom where he slept soundly.

"Even if I do say so, I did a pretty good job of putting that boy back together that night," Albrecht said with a smile. "But then, you know, I had help. I went into my private office and prayed to God that He help this child to live. And He did. When the boy recovered, I gave him the

Popeye doll, and that was what he remembered of the event. He wasn't much to look at, but he wasn't dead, either. God had guided me in my first attempt at brain surgery."

Such has been the wellspring of Albrecht's life. From the faith sown in his youth, he has always known and acknowledged the source of his successes and the balm for his failures. When Margery, learning eagerly about his past, asked him how he managed to accomplish so much, he wordlessly raised his index finger heavenward. It was his answer to her question and to his entire life.

Recounting his career to Margery has become an absorbing litany for both Albrechts. The story is an amazing one: healing for more than fifty years, creating almost single-handedly a health program that restored a people and nurtured a state, serving under seven governors, receiving two honorary doctorate degrees, strengthening higher education both in and outside Alaska, helping to win modern hospital care for Alaska Natives and at-home care for the mentally ill, founding a flourishing circumpolar effort against disease—and those are only part of the record.

One small entry in that record is nevertheless among Albrecht's proudest—undoubtedly because it occurred at Bethel but also because it epitomized his hopes for his battle against tuberculosis. It happened after a service at the Moravian Church one Sunday in 1953. Mrs. Ferdinand Drebert, wife of the minister, sought out Albrecht among the parishioners. She had a special message for him.

"We know your health program is working," she told him, "because our children are no longer dying of TB. Look," she said, pointing to a batch of giggling youngsters, spilling out of the church, "now, for the first time, our church school is growing."

Albrecht turned, saw the healthy children, heard the happy noise. Amen, he thought, amen.

# Bibliography

PERSONAL PAPERS

The C. Earl and Margery J. Albrecht Collection, Bradenton, Florida.

The Albrecht Collection, University of Alaska Anchorage Archives, Anchorage, Alaska.

INTERVIEWS

Dr. C. Earl Albrecht, Margery J. Albrecht, Robert B. Atwood, Lucille Ring Bear, Elsie Havens Blue, Ruth Kelly Coffey, Dr. Robert Fortuine, Catherine Smulling Gair, Dr. Leo J. Gehrig, William Graffius, Dr. Carl Hild, Miriam Hilscher, Lois Jund, Claire Kipperud, Kay Linton, Mary Bagoy Lakshas, Dr. and Mrs. Frederick P. McGinnis, Dr. John Middaugh, Stella Odsather, Dr. Frank Pauls, Max Sherrod, Dr. Robert Smith, Gertrude Albrecht Teufer, Dr. Elizabeth Tower.

ORAL HISTORY TRANSCRIPTS

Oral History Collection of the Alaska and Polar Regions Department, Elmer E. Rasmuson Library, University of Alaska Fairbanks, Fairbanks, Alaska:

> Interview with C.E. Albrecht—Kenneth G. Kastella, 1983
> Interview with C.E. Albrecht—Daniel O'Neill, 1986
> "The Scientists": Robert Forbes, William Mills, M.D., Kenelm Philip, Leslie A. Viereck, Gunter Weller, 1987.

C. Earl and Margery J. Albrecht Collection, Bradenton, Florida:

> Recollections by C. Earl Albrecht of World War II.

BOOKS

Cloe, John Haile. *The Aleutian Warriors: A History of the 11th Air Force and Fleet Air.* Missoula, Montana: Pictorial Histories Publishing Co., 1990.

Davis, Neil. *The College Hill Chronicles: How the University of Alaska Came of Age.* Fairbanks, Alaska: University of Alaska Foundation, 1990.

Denison, B.W. *Alaska Today.* Caldwell, Idaho: Caxton Printers, 1949.

Fortuine, Robert. *Alaska Native Medical Center: A History, 1953-1983.* Anchorage, Alaska: Alaska Native Medical Center/Indian Health Service, 1986.

Fortuine, Robert. *Chills and Fever: Health and Disease in the Early History of Alaska.* Fairbanks, Alaska: University of Alaska Press, 1989.

Garfield, Brian. *The 1000-Mile War: World War II in Alaska and the Aleutians.* Garden City, New York: Doubleday, 1969.

Mills, Stephen E. *Arctic War Birds: Alaska Aviation in World War II.* Seattle, Washington: Superior Publishing Co., 1971.

"The capture of Attu as told by the men who fought there." U.S. War Department, Washington, D.C. *The Infantry Journal,* 1944.

*Circumpolar Health 74 Proceedings of the 3rd International Symposium on Circumpolar Health.* Yellowknife, Northwest Territories, 1974. Roy J. Shepard and S. Itoh, Editors. Toronto, Ontario: University of Toronto Press, 1976.

*Circumpolar Health 81 Proceedings of the 5th International Symposium on Circumpolar Health.* Copenhagen, Denmark, August 9-13, 1981. Bent Harvald and J.P. Hart Hansen, Editors. Oulu, Finland: Nordic Council for Arctic Medical Research, 1982.

*Circumpolar Health 84 Proceedings of the 6th International Symposium on Circumpolar Health.* Anchorage, Alaska, May 13-18, 1984. Robert Fortuine, Editor. Seattle, Washington: University of Washington Press, 1985.

*Circumpolar Health 1987 Proceedings of the 7th International Symposium on Circumpolar Health.* Umea, Sweden, June 8-12, 1987. Hakan Linderholm, Christer Backman, Noel Broadbent, Ingemar Joelsson, Editors. Oulu, Finland: Nordic Council for Medical Research, 1988.

*Circumpolar Health 90 Proceedings of the 8th International Congress on Circumpolar Health.* Whitehorse, Yukon, May 20-25, 1990. Brian Postl, Penny Gilbert, Jean Goodwill, Michael E.K. Moffatt, John D. O'Neil, Peter A. Sarsfield, T.Kue Young, Editors. Winnipeg, Manitoba: University of Manitoba Press, 1991.

*Alaska's Health, A Survey Report to the United States Department of the Interior by the Alaska Health Survey Team.* Thomas Parran, Chief; Max Q. Edler, Editor. (The Parran Report) Pittsburgh, Pennsylvania: The Graduate School of Public Health, University of Pittsburgh, 1954.

PUBLICATIONS

Newspapers: *Palmer Daily,* Palmer, Alaska; *Akron Beacon Journal,* Akron, Ohio; *Anchorage Daily Times,* Anchorage, Alaska; *Cleveland News,* Cleveland, Ohio; *Cleveland Plain Dealer,* Cleveland, Ohio; *Columbus Citizen,* Columbus, Ohio; *Fairbanks Daily News-Miner,* Fairbanks, Alaska; *Juneau Empire,* Juneau, Alaska; *Juneau Independent,* Juneau, Alaska.

Health departments' monthly publications: *Alaska Health,* Juneau, Alaska; *Motive,* Columbus, Ohio.

# Index

# About the Author

When Nancy Jordan was given a child's printing set at age 10, she put out regular editions of a neighborhood newspaper and has been playing with the printed word ever since.

While attending Boston University, she was university correspondent for four Boston newspapers and then became assistant managing editor of the Newport (R.I.) *Daily News.* Following a year with a Boston publisher, she became education writer for the Providence (R.I.) *Journal Bulletin*, where she met and married John Strohmeyer, a fellow reporter. After her marriage she was assistant director of the Brown University News Bureau.

When her husband was named editor of the Bethlehem (Pa.) *Globe-Times*, she became director of the news bureau for Moravian College and wrote for local newspapers. She also authored a history of Pennsylvania's Northampton County and contributed to a history of the city of Bethlehem.

When the Strohmeyers came to Anchorage, Alaska, in 1987, she joined the staff of *The Anchorage Times* as theater reviewer and arts/features writer. Later she was copy editor for Alaska Newspapers, Inc. She has been adjunct professor of journalism at the University of Alaska Anchorage.

The Strohmeyers are parents of two sons and one daughter, all of whom they have taught to fish, and have seven grandchildren, who are in the process of learning.

# Other Biographies from Epicenter Press

## TALES OF ALASKA'S BUSH RAT GOVERNOR

### Jay Hammond

This fast-paced, often hilarious autobiography is the odyssey of a man who became the nation's most besieged but effective environmentalist governor during Alaska's oil-boom years.
$27.95 hardbound, 352 pages, 50 B&W photos

## FLYING COLD
## The Adventures of Russel Merrill, Pioneer Alaskan Aviator

### Robert Merrill MacLean and Sean Rossiter

Trained as a pilot during World War I, Russel Merrill's love of flight lured him to Alaska, where he became a pioneer of commercial aviation.
$34.95 hardbound; $24.95 softbound
192 pages, 75 B&W photos, maps and illustrations

## CARMACK OF THE KLONDIKE

### James Albert Johnson

The story of a prospector with determination, luck, and a secret past who touched off the world's greatest gold rush—a remarkable biography drawn from letters spanning forty years of George Washington Carmack's life.
$14.95 softbound, 176 pages, 24 B&W photos

## ART AND ESKIMO POWER
## The Life and Times of Alaskan Howard Rock

### Lael Morgan

Prior to Howard Rock's birth in 1911 in a remote Eskimo village, a shaman predicted that Rock would become a great man. This biography of one of America's great Eskimo journalists and political activists chronicles the fulfillment of that prophecy.
Retail Price: $24.95 hardbound; $16.95 softbound
260 pages, 30 B&W photos

To find a copy of any of these biographies, visit your favorite bookstore. Many booksellers will help with special orders. Or, send a check for the purchase price (plus 8.2% sales tax on orders from Washington state) and $3 for postage and handling to: Epicenter Press, Box 82368, Kenmore, WA 98028. Visa/MC orders may be phoned to 206-485-6822, or faxed to 206-481-8253.